A NEW DIVAN

Other books of interest published by Gingko

The West-Eastern Divan
Johann Wolfgang von Goethe
Translated and annotated by Eric Ormsby

Hafiz, Goethe and the Gingko
Inspirations for The New Divan 2015–2019

A NEW DIVAN

A lyrical dialogue between
East & West

Edited by
Barbara Schwepcke and Bill Swainson

GINGKO

First published in Great Britain by
Gingko
4 Molasses Row, Plantation Wharf
London SW11 3UX

Supported using public funding by

**ARTS COUNCIL
ENGLAND**

LOTTERY FUNDED

Supported by the Stiftung-Gingko Library

HB ISBN 978-1-909942-28-8
eBook ISBN 978-1-909942-29-5

10 9 8 7 6 5 4 3 2 1

Designed and typeset in Minion by Libanus Press
Printed in Great Britain by Clays Ltd, Elcograf S.p.A.

In Memory of Mark Linz

Gingko Biloba

The Gingko, that Eastern tree,
In my garden plot now grows.
In its leaf there seems to be
A secret that the wise man knows.

Is that leaf one and lonely?
In itself in two divided?
Is it two that have decided
To be seen as one leaf only?

To such questions I reply:
Do not my love songs say to you
– Should you ever wonder why
I sing, that I am one yet two?

Translated from the German by Anthea Bell

CONTENTS

ESSAYS

Hafiz, Goethe and *A New Divan*

It all started with Goethe's poem 'Gingko Biloba', which the late Anthea Bell beautifully translated in memory of Werner Mark Linz when the pain felt at the loss of this inspirational man was still raw, and which appears as the epigraph to this book.

Johann Wolfgang von Goethe sent this poem to his beloved friend Marianne von Willemer as a token of his affection. He pasted two dried, crossed leaves from this ancient tree below the three stanzas and dated it 15 September 1815. Goethe, Germany's greatest poet and polymath, natural scientist, statesman and true cosmopolite, had picked the Gingko leaf as a symbol of hope, long life and, above all, deep affection. The poem was his ode to friendship and symbolised the union between old and young, man and woman, human and the Divine, literature and scholarship, East and West – a union which in his mind was inseparable.

The poem became part of his *West-Eastern Divan*, which Goethe was inspired to write when he read the first German translation of the *divan* composed by the fourteenth-century Persian poet Hafiz. Goethe called Hafiz his 'twin' and decided to enter into a lyrical dialogue with 'the Other'. In Islamic cultures *divan* means a collection of poems and Goethe proceeded to assemble his own *divan* of twelve books of poetry, calling them *nameh,* the Persian word for 'epic poem'. He added a second part, 'Notes and Essays for a Better Understanding of the *West-Eastern Divan*', which included a section on a 'Prospective Divan'. Considering his own *Divan* 'incomplete', it was his suggestion of how a *divan* might be attempted by poets and scholars of the future.

The *West-Eastern Divan*, published in 1819, was Goethe's very personal attempt to broaden the horizons of readers both ignorant and fearful of the Islamic world. From the time of the Persian Wars the

Orient had been seen as alien, as a threat to the West – a threat, however, that was central to the formation of Western identity.

Two empty chairs, cut from one single block of granite, stand in Weimar, facing each other. They represent Goethe and Hafiz, divided by centuries and cultures, but united by poetry, which is woven into the carpet-like bronze base. The German president Joachim Rau, who with his Iranian counterpart Mohammad Khatami inaugurated the monument, chose the following lines from the *West-Eastern Divan*:

> *Know yourself and in that instant*
> *Know the Other and see therefore*
> *Orient and Occident*
> *Cannot be parted for ever more*

'To everything there is a season!' These words from the Book of Ecclesiastes open the scholarly essays that form part of the *West-Eastern Divan*. Today we face another era in which the West feels threatened by Islam, by the 'Other', by the unknown, which, whilst understanding very little about what this means, is all too often equated with religious fundamentalism. 'To everything there is a season!', Goethe said, and the season now seems right to attempt a *divan* for our times: a *New Divan*.

Thus, on 15 September 2015 – exactly two hundred years after Goethe sent his poem to Marianne – flanked by Narguess Farzad and Joachim Sartorius, my advisors of the first hour, I outlined the roadmap of this ambitious endeavour. I mainly addressed my words to people in the audience without whom this project would never have come to fruition: Bill Swainson, my co-editor of this volume, and Mena Mark Hanna, the Dean of the Barenboim–Said Akademie in Berlin, where the two-hundredth anniversary celebrations will culminate.

We would invite twenty-four leading poets – twelve from the 'East' and twelve from the 'West' – to metaphorically take a seat on the empty chairs in Weimar and continue the lyrical dialogue Goethe started with Hafiz 200 years ago. In addition six essayists would be invited to explore the differences and similarities between Eastern and Western poetry and discuss the challenges of literary and cultural translation. Their contributions to this volume enhance and complement the poems, and mirror Goethe's original 'Notes and Essays for a Better Understanding of the *West-Eastern Divan*'.

On the two-hundredth anniversary of the publication of the *West-Eastern Divan*, the 'Dichter und Denker', the poets, scholars and translators, will assemble at the Barenboim–Said Akademie in Berlin for a three-day festival; Gingko will not only bring out a new bilingual edition of the *West-Eastern Divan* but also this volume, of which the German edition is published by Suhrkamp. The festival will be a celebration of poetry and music, drawing on the interwoven traditions of one art form inspiring the other and one culture enriching another. It is our firm hope that *A New Divan* will continue the mission of the *West-Eastern Divan*, that of trying to bridge the perceived divide between Orient and Occident. The greatest accolade of the two-hundredth anniversary of the *West-Eastern Divan*, however, would be if this lyrical dialogue, which Goethe started with Hafiz, were to continue for another 200 years.

Barbara Haus Schwepcke
London, 18 March 2019

FOREWORD

Daniel Barenboim

Und wo sich die Völker trennen
Gegenseitig im Verachten,
Keins von beiden wird bekennen,
Dass sie nach demselben trachten.

And when people are divided by mutual contempt, neither
will acknowledge that they are striving for the same thing.*

It is hard to imagine a sentiment more appropriate and fitting for the
conflict between the Israeli and Palestinian peoples than this one
expressed by Johann Wolfgang von Goethe in his *West-Eastern Divan*.
At its heart, the conflict is, after all, not a political conflict but a deeply
human one – between two groups of people whose destinies are inex-
tricably linked and who themselves are entirely convinced that they
are entitled to live on the same small piece of land, preferably without
the other. When Edward Said and I founded the West-Eastern Divan
Orchestra in 1999, twenty years ago in Weimar, Germany, we did not
have the lofty goal of creating an orchestra that would bring about
peace between those two peoples. Rather, we set out to create an
independent space in which Israeli and Arab musicians could come
together to debate, argue and reconcile their diverging experiences
and opinions – and most of all, to find commonality in a shared goal:
that of making music together to the highest possible standard.

This reimagining of Goethe's seminal work gives us the opportun-
ity to re-engage with his thoughts – a much needed exercise, given
the state of the world today. Goethe's own experiences in Weimar in

* Johann Wolfgang von Goethe, Poem 69, The Book of Ill-Humour, *West-Eastern
Divan*, translated and annotated by Eric Ormsby (London: Gingko, 2019), p. 125.

the early nineteenth century, prior to writing the bulk of the *West-Eastern Divan*, mirror what many Arabs must have felt at the height of colonialism and since: a sentiment of impotence vis-à-vis a more modern and better-structured military power – in Goethe's case, Napoleon's *grande armée* – invading previously autonomous societies. Goethe's poems speak of oriental and occidental cultures, of East and West in equally respectful measure. His key message remains one not of division, but of mutual respect and cultural dialogue based on the recognition that we all share the same universal human roots.

As Goethe says, most people, in essence, long for the same things: peace, prosperity, happiness, self-fulfilment among them. Twenty years of working together in the West-Eastern Divan Orchestra have shown us, again and again, that our commonalities can outweigh our differences, no matter how existential they seem. Goethe has not only given the orchestra its name, he has also given it its deep-rooted philosophy:

> Wer sich selbst und andere kennt,
> wird auch hier erkennen:
> Orient und Okzident
> nicht mehr zu trennen.[*]

We hope that this *New Divan* created by twenty-four poets from East and West, will help impart Goethe's wisdom to people everywhere. From our own experience, we know just how powerful it can be.

Daniel Barenboim
6 March 2019, Berlin

---

[*] Whoever knows himself and others will recognise this too: Orient and Occident are no longer to be separated. Poem 241, Appendix: Poems Collected Posthumously, *West Eastern Divan*, p. 577.

Mariam C. Said

Edward Said, a Palestinian met Daniel Barenboim, an Israeli by chance. They became friends and broke the barriers that separated them. They recorded their conversations in a book titled, *Parallels and Paradoxes*.

In 1999 Weimar was designated Cultural Capital of Europe. In telling the story of the musical workshop that took place at Weimar, Edward wrote 'Daniel was offered the chance to perform in Weimar . . . I happened to be there and so was YoYo Ma.' The three of them had a brief discussion and decided to do something different, a workshop of young Arab and Israeli musicians. The organisers of the events were delighted.

The musicians that were selected proved to be very competent and Daniel made an orchestra out of the group. They called the orchestra 'The West-Eastern Divan' in honour of Goethe.

Describing the workshop in a lecture a few years later Edward wrote: 'In Weimar . . . figuratively speaking we were under the wing of Goethe, Weimar's most famous inhabitant, who had written there his great mature masterpiece the *West-östlicher Divan*, an extraordinary act of homage to Islam generally, and to Hafiz in particular. Goethe was, I believe, the first great modern European to attempt some kind of artistic synthesis and involvement between what in those days were called 'The Orient' and Europe. His accomplishment was the magnificent *Divan* itself, as well as for our purposes the use of art, so to speak, to create an imaginative re-ordering of polarities, differences and oppositions, on the basis not of politics but of affinities, spiritual generosity and aesthetic self-renewal . . .' He goes on to say 'The point of all this is that a new paradigm emerged for us and our students who were, it should go without saying, from differing and sometimes jarringly antagonistic backgrounds and whose interests, ambitions, histories and commitments during the three weeks were suspended, as it were, in the interests of music.'*

That was the beginning of an educational, musical and humanistic endeavor. It allowed the participants to know 'the Other' as equal through music and to learn to think in alternate ways. Twenty years later the Divan orchestra is thriving, proving its founders' vision and attesting Goethe's belief that the East and West complement each other.

Mariam C. Said
New York, 27 February 2019

---

* Extracted from 'Memory, Inequality, and Power: Palestine and the Universality of Human Rights', an unpublished lecture given by Edward Said in January 2003 at SOAS, University of London, sponsored by Sir Joseph Hotung, Project in Law, Human Rights and Peace Building in the Middle East.

POEMS

أدونيس

رسالة إلى غوته

في الظّهيرة، أيقَظتُ ليلَيَ باسمِكَ، أصغَيْتُ:
دبُّ الكواكبِ يُمْلي على الدّورةِ الدّمَويّةِ في الأرضِ آياتِه.
والمَدائنُ – مختومةٌ   بشَمْعِ الشّرائعِ، تقرأُ أسفارَها
على بَشَرٍ من جِراحٍ وخُبْزٍ   يَطوفونَ
يستفسرونَ الشّوارعَ: من أينَ جِئنا
إلى أينَ نمضي؟ وهذا
قمَرُ الشّرقِ يدخُل في طَقْسِه.

أهُوَ الوَقْتُ، يا نبْعَ حرّيّتي؟
سأتابعُ سَيْري.
أهُوَ الشّرقُ ينأى عن الغربِ، يُعطي سماواتِه،
إلى قمرٍ آخَرٍ؟
سأتابعُ سيري.
كلُّ شيءٍ مَجازٌ –
ليسَتِ الرّوحُ إلّا مَنيّاً له صورتانْ
صورةٌ ترسمُ الزّمانَ بحِبْرِ غواياتِها،
صورةٌ تلبسُ المَكانْ.

إنه الغَرْبُ خلفَكَ، والشّرقُ ليس أمامي.
ضِفّتانِ لنَهْرٍ
واحِدٍ صار أكثرَ من هُوّةٍ
وأكثرَ من صَخْرةٍ
ليس سيزيفُ إلّا صوتَها صارخاً:
سِندَبادٌ يتشَرّدُ في بَحْرِ إسلامِه
ماتَ جلجامِشٌ، وعوليسُ في مَوْجِه.

ADONIS

Letter To Goethe

English translation from the Arabic by Khaled Mattawa

In the afternoon, I conjured my night in your name, and listened to
    the Great Bear dictate his   verses to earth's blood flow,
    and to the cities, sealed with the wax of laws, recite their scrolls
    to people made of wounds and bread   who roam
    asking the streets: Where did we come from?
    Where do we go? And now
    The moon of the East resumes its rituals.

Is it time, dear spring of my freedom?
    I'll go on walking.
Is the East veering away from the West, offering its heavens
    to another moon?
I'll go on walking.
Everything is allowed –
       The soul is nothing but sperm that appears in two guises:
       One image depicts time with the ink of its temptations.
       Another apprehends space.

The West is behind you, but the East is not before me.
      They are two banks of one river.
      One has become more than an abyss,
      more than a rock;
      Sisyphus is its voice screaming:
Sinbad wanders the sea of his Islam,
Gilgamesh is dead, and Ulysses is lost among his waves.

جسدٌ واحدٌ يتمزّقُ عُضواً فَعُضواً
جسدٌ ليس فيه من الشّرقِ إلاّ اسمُهُ.
جسدٌ ليس فيه من الغربِ إلاّ اسمُهُ.

لم أعُدْ أتَعَدّدُ مثلَكَ، في وحدةٍ أتَنَشَّقُ إكسيرَها وأناجي أنابيقَها
لم أعُدْ قادِراً أن أُميّزَ مثلَكَ: مَن هو قابيلُ؟
مَن هو هابيلُ؟ كلاّ،
لا ترى خطواتيَ
في غابةِ الكَوْنِ ما يتوهّجُ فيها

ما يُضيءُ مسافاتِها،
ويُجَدّدُ أبعادَها.
أتُرى أوّلُ الشّرقِ غَرْبٌ؟
أتُرى آخِرُ الغربِ شرقٌّ؟

هكذا أفْتَحُ الكلِماتِ على جُرْحِ هذا الوجودِ، على هَوْله
وأرى كيف يجْتاحُني
وأرى كيف يجتاحُ شطآنَ حُبّي
ويَسْتَدرِجُ الأشرعهْ
للذهاب إلى آخِرِ المَوْجِ غَرْباً وشَرْقاً، إلى آخِرِ الظّلُماتِ،
إلى ما يُسَمّيه نفسي
وإلى ما يؤكّدُ أنّي ضدّ نفسي، مَعَهْ.

الأساطيرُ في الغربِ والشّرقِ مَجروحةٌ
وأنا لسْتُ إلاّ دماً
يتقطّرُ مِنها.

One body is ripped limb by limb:
A body that has no East except its name,
A body that has no West except its name.

I no longer multiply like you. I live in solitude whose elixir I inhale and
    whose alembics I beseech.
Unlike you, I can no longer distinguish: Who is Cain?
    Who is Abel? No, my steps do not see
        through the forest of the universe what flashes there,

what lights its distances
and renews its magnitude.
Do you think the beginning of the East is West?
Do you think the end of the West is East?

This is how I open words to reveal the wound of creation, to witness
    its enormity.
    I see it invade me
    and I see how it overruns the shores of my love,
    how it lures the sails
    toward the ends of the waves, West and East, to the ends of darkness,
to what it names as myself,
to what confirms that I am allied with it, against myself.

Myths in the West and East are wounded.
    I am only blood
    dripping from them.

KHALED MATTAWA

Easter Sunday, Rajab in Mid-Moon

Find the poet   by the Channel of Mozambique
flown South to taste the air   of the first migrants
Khidr's progeny   canoeing from the other side of earth.

He's come to submit   to heaven's teachings   to study
the clouds' wide belief   the rains' narrow thoughts
to mirror his talismans on Isalo's lagoons.   Find the poet

in a steely howdah   all-drive wheels.   The stars'
algorithms spin his many destinies   same looms
that map land and sea   gouge the hills out of cobalt

where the crust softens to a sponge of undrinkable brine.
Shacks of galvanise encircle him   taut-limbed women
buckets on their heads   babies wrapped to their ribs

bare feet that walk carless roads.   Scenery as if taken
from ancient footage.   Our onlooker rides an engine
that could suffice a village's need for light   spends enough

to build a school.   Why is he here?   The zebu he's eaten
could be the last of the herd.   What is he but a sign
unattainable   his living other than a gloomy striving?

Remnants of scorched dirt fields   of 'harvested' woods
leave him like a sperm   around a crowd of his own   ravenous
with nothing to attach himself to.   What does love mean

in a time of love unspirited?   he asks,   the body a rope
of flesh and words   pulse of the sun's touch –   how vision
was merely skin once   he recalls   how once upon a time

we caught the scent of poppies with our hands.   How can he
sing his gratitude?   What origins to seek now?   Must he
still praise the living who long for death in flame?

عباس بيضون

زليخا و مارلين

من قلب البئر صعد صوتي، والذئب الّذي إخترعوه لي، سمعني وهرب
القميص الّذي بللوه بدم كاذب أعشى عيني أبي
هل كان البئر حقيقيًا، هل كان القميص حقيقيا؟
هل صدقت الصحراء، هل صدق الذّئب؟
ما الّذي كان ينتظرني عند فم البئر؟
سوى طريق الأنبياء إلى مصر

في كتاب قديم وجدت أنا الشاعر بلاطا و ملكة وسجنا
الجميلة الّتي أحبّت يوسف قطعت أصابعها من أجله
ليس أقلّ من دم حقيقي هذه المرّة، ليس أقلّ من قميص حقيقي
أنا الشاعر لا أجد دما لقصيدتي، بريت أصابعي لأكتبها
وجدت زليخا في مخيّم للنازحين تحمل مكواة حامية
أحرقت أصابعها وقرّحتها
صورة أخيها الميّت معلّقة على الحائط
أنا الشاعر أعرف أنّها نزفت من يديها، وهي تجلي، فوق الصحون
أن جمالها مطموس في أسمالها

ABBAS BEYDOUN

Suleika and Marilyn

English version by Bill Manhire,
based on a literal translation from the Arabic by Reem Ghanayem

I heard myself call from deep in the well.
The wolf my brothers invented, he listened and fled.
It wasn't my blood on the shirt, but still our father was blinded.
Was there a real well? A real shirt?
Was the desert a true place? Was the wolf himself actual?
What awaited me up on the earth's surface
but the Prophets' Road to Egypt?

In an ancient book
I found a court, a queen, a keep.
Suleika loved Yusuf and cut her fingers . . .
Oh, real blood that time; a real shirt, too.

I am searching for blood for my poem.
My fingers grow sharp as I write it.
I find Suleika in a refugee camp.
The hot iron she carries
burns and blisters her fingers.
On the wall, a photo of her dead brother;
I can see how her hands bleed as she does the dishes,
how her beauty is there in the rags she wears.

أفكّر الآن بمارلين مونرو الّتي إنتحرت من شقاء العالم
وصعوبة الحبّ
لقد أشرقت على ملايين غادروا الصالات وإنصرفوا إلى أعمالهم
قالوا أنّها مختلّة، إنتظروا جميعا أن تنضج لتستحقّهم

أنا الشاعر، أعرف أنّي لست كحافظ ولا سعدي ولا المتنبي ولا جلال الدّين الرومي
اولئك تطلّعوا إلى ما يجعلهم أعلى من أنفسهم، إلى تجربة كونيّة
كانوا يتّصلون بالكون عن طريق الحب، كانوا يسمعون النجوم عن طريق الحب
الشعراء اليوم مساجين في غرف الآلات
هم وحدهم ونساؤهم من ورق
العالم ينتكس، وأنفسنا تنتكس معه، إنّها تنظر فقط إلى ما هو أدنى منها
ثمنها الوحيد هو الموت، الإنتحار من أجل لا شيء، في عالم لم يعد له سعر
زليخا في البلاط إنتظرت شيئا أعلى من تاج، شيئا أكثر من ملك
الجمال السماوي الّذي جاء من بئر في الصحراء كان أصيلا وكونيّا
يوسف الّذي لم يأكله الذّئب ولا الصحراء رأى ما وراء النجوم
زليخا بأصابعها المقطوعة، المزهرة والمضيئة، لامست السماء

ماذا تفعل أيّها الشاعر العجوز، أنت الّذي لا يقطفك أحد
حتّى متى تنتظر زليخا
لقد واكبت مارلين إلى القبر
وعمّا قريب في مكان آخر ستقع في الحفرة
بدون هدف، ولن يخرجك أحد من البئر
إنّه موعدك مع اللاأحد

And now I am thinking of Marilyn Monroe.
She took her life because the world is made of pain
plus tiny scraps of love. She shone high on the screen
and a million men returned to their lives. Ah, they said,
is she quite stable? One day she will surely grow up
and acknowledge our worth!

I am just a little voice. Hafiz, Saadi, Rumi, Mutanabbi . . .
they sang beyond themselves, their embrace went wide.
Love held them up to the universe,
they listened to the stars. These days
poets are locked in their machines,
each one alone with a woman made of paper.
Ours is an age that drifts and slides, and we go with it;
we seek small things that never mattered,
find suicide and death in a world without worth.
Suleika waited for more than a crown, a king.
True divinity came from that well in the desert.
Yusuf, who survived the wolf, saw beyond the stars.
Suleika's fingers flowered and flamed and touched the sky.

And you, what will you do, old fellow, old poet,
you whom no one has use for?
How long must Suleika wait?
Marilyn moves towards her grave.
Soon and in another place you will plunge
deep into the earth and thus beyond all purpose,
and no one there to lift you back to the surface.
Oh this is your date with no one.

DURS GRÜNBEIN

Der Teufel im Orient

1

Groß in Mode heute ist das Kampfwort: Lüge.
Presse lügt und Fernsehn lügt, und Politik
Gilt als Spiel, die Wähler zu betrügen.
Es herrscht Krieg, wie immer, und der Trick:
Die Verwirrung aller. Freund und Feind
Sind im Sumpf der Niedertracht vereint.
Chuzpe pur: ein Wort wie Auschwitz-Lüge.

Fake news sagt man: Keim für den Verdacht,
Daß da etwas, Wahrheit, nicht mehr stimmt.
Autokraten, Oligarchen, Präsidenten – Macht
Hat, wer im Strom der Lügen oben schwimmt.
Fakten-Fälschung… Geld verzerrt die Maße.
Info heißt der Irrsinn, die Statistik wird getürkt.
Und die Haßparolen ziehen durch die Straßen.

Hashtag Lüge. Das Gerücht regiert, infam.
Schwer mißbrauchte Worte, die ein jeder kennt:
Freiheit, Glaube, Sicherheit – und keine Scham.
Lüge, Lüge, wiederholt wird festes Fundament
(Demagogen-Theorem). So geht das, so

DURS GRÜNBEIN

The Devil in the Orient

English version by Matthew Sweeney,
based on a literal translation from the German by Karen Leeder

1

What's in, boys, at the moment, is the slogan: *Lie!*
The newspapers lie, the TV lies, and politics
has become a game of duping the voters, yeah!
War is the master, as ever, and the trick
is the disarray of everyone. Friend and enemy
are brought together in a morass of perfidy.
Pure chutzpah – reminds me of the Auschwitz lie.

Fake news they scream: germ for the suspicion
that truth is the one thing we no longer buy.
Autocrats, oligarchs, presidents, all the big players –
power goes to the top swimmer in the stream of lies.
The adulteration of facts . . . Money fiddles the figures.
This lunacy is called info, the statistics are jiggled
and the hate-banners are carried through the streets.

Lie is the hashtag. Rumour rules the roost!
Badly misused words that everyone knows:
Freedom, belief, safety – shameless!
To lie, lie repeatedly is the only way to go.
(Demagogue's theorem). That's how it happens, how

Setzt ein Wort die halbe Welt in Brand: Islam.
Sprache, Täuschung, war von Anfang an.
Alle lügen und die Dichter sowieso.

2

Es regnet, es plattert
Auf die Kameltreiberstadt.
Wer läßt es regnen? Der Teufel.
Wer läßt die Fladen
Von schwarzem Kameldung
Auf die Häupter der Gläubigen
Herunterklatschen,
Allah, Deus, Jehova?

Tage, Wochen und Jahre
Habe ich ausgeharrt.
Auf die eine Zeile wartend,
Die den monotonen Regen
Des Monotheismus
In aller Stille, den Mäusen,
Schmetterlingen und Spatzen –
Allen zarten Wesen,
Den Tieren und Kindern
Zuliebe beendet.

a word sets half the world on fire: Islam.
Language, subterfuge was there from the start.
Everyone lies, and the poets in any event.

2

It's raining, it's pouring
onto the camel-drovers' town.
Who authorised the rain? The devil.
Who allows the pancakes
of black camel dung
to parachute down onto
the heads of the believers?
Allah? Deus? Jehovah?

Days, weeks, even years
I have held out,
waiting for the one line
which will end the monotonous rain
of belief in the one god,
and this is secretly for the mice,
the butterflies, the sparrows –
all gentle beings,
the animals and children,
and that's the last word.

3

In Samarkand, in Samarkand
Saß er im Burnus vor lehmgelber Wand.

In den staubigen Straßen im Morgenland
Blieb er als Einziger unerkannt.

Durch Basare voller berauschendem Tand
War es, daß er am Mittag verschwand

Zwischen den Eselkarren am Straßenrand,
Den Rosenkranz in der linken Hand.

Der Fleck aber sah aus wie abgebrannt,
Was niemand dort sonderbar fand.

3

In Samarkand, in Samarkand
he sat in a burnous with his back to a yellow earth wall.

In the dusty streets of the Morning-land
he was the one unrecognised man.

Through bazaars of exhilarating geegaws
he absconded, as the clock rang out noon,

past donkey carts lining the dirt road,
a rosary beads draped on his left hand.

But where he'd sat looked burned down,
which nobody there found uncommon.

إيمان مرسال

رائحتك تراب العالم

ينادي البائع، على أسماك لم تعد تنتمي للبحر،
أمرّ على رائحة ملح وحبال غسيل، أمرُّ بلابسات السواد
على باب المستشفى، أمام دكان الجيش ومحكمة الأسرة.
نهنهة مكتومة أم دعاء؟
بعد شارعين سأصعد السلالم إليك.
وعَدَني الصباح بجريمةٍ وصدقته.

هويّتي على ممسحة الأحذية أمام الباب.
لا حاجة لاسمي، غسلتُ رأسي وتركتها تجفّ على فرع شجرة
ستخلعها عاصفة بعد قليل.
أنا ما تبقّى من ذلك،
أمشي في اتجاهك بعينين مغمضتين، وأعرف، لن أكون هنا ولا هناك
عندما تطفو ذاكرتي نفسها في نهر النسيان.

لسنوات أرعى الغنم، مع ذلك نزفت قدماي إلى المدينة،
المدينة التي نجوتَ من حربها الأهليّة وما زالت الجثثَ في المرآة.
أنا عمياء وأنت لا تريد أن ترى
نصل إلى اللحظة من طريقين متقابلين
الرغبة كالماء.
تُبَلّل وتروي وتُغرق وتميت، ولا يمكن مسكها بالأصابع.

لا أخاف من كتفي الأيمن ولا من كتفي الأيسر ولا من نقطة العرق بين ثديي.
لا أخاف من ذاكرة السُّرّة ولا الشامة على الرقبة
ولا الجرح القديم في الرّكبة ولا أظافر قدميّ.

IMAN MERSAL

Your Smell Is the World's Dust

English version by Elaine Feinstein,
based on a literal translation from the Arabic by Robyn Creswell

The fish the seller is touting no longer belong to the sea.
I smell salt and lines of washing as I pass the women in black
in front of the hospital, the army store and the family courts.
Is that a repressed sob or a cry?
No matter: two streets more and I'll climb the steps to you.
Morning promised wickedness, and I believed it.

I have left my identity card on the doormat.
No need of my name. I have washed my head and put it out to dry
on the branch of a tree which a storm will soon uproot –
I am no more than what remains after that,
moving towards you with my eyes tight shut.
It's not important where I float on this river of forgetting.

Once I herded livestock and wore out my feet to reach the city
and that civil war you escaped, though you still see corpses in your mirror.
Now I am blind and you do not wish to see
as we move towards the moment our paths come together.
Desire is like water. It irrigates and drowns.
We can never grasp it with our fingers.

What happens to my shoulders or the sweat between my breasts doesn't
    frighten me,
I'm not afraid of what my navel remembers, or that birthmark on the neck
nor the old wound on my knee. Nor toenails!

يُمكنك أن تُصوّر كل عضو وحده،
أظلّ عندك كثيرة ومتناثرة، كل عضو سيدلّ عليّ،
بينما عيناي التي شهدت كل شيء، معي، تحدق في الداخل.

ملاءة السرير المطرزة بالورود تملؤها الأشواك.
ليس في الأمر مجاز.
نحن بشرٌ للغاية، لا نحلم بالطيران.
النوم بجانبك أشبه بالرجوع للأرض،
ورائحتك تراب العالم.

سيجارة في غبشة النوم
رحلة الضباب تلك
التي يفشل في وصفها العائدون من الموت.

If all our limbs were scattered I would still remain with you,
and every limb of yours would point to me.
My eyes, which have seen everything, look only inward.

The bed sheets are embroidered with roses covered in thorns
and there is no metaphor in writing that.
We are all too human; we do not dream of flight.
Sleeping beside you is like returning to the earth
and your smell is that of the world's soil,

or a cigarette in the twilight of sleep
on a journey through fog
which those who return from the dead can never describe.

HOMERO ARIDJIS

La creación del mundo por los animales

(según el *Popol Vuh*)

el cielo estaba vacío y sin movimiento
y la guacamaya escarlata fue un rayo de colores
en la oscuridad uniforme
y las oropéndolas de ojos de azul turquesa
comenzaron a tocar en la mañana
el solo de la luz

en la ceiba prodigiosa, madre de pájaros,
apareció el esquelético mono araña,
con sus genitales colgando, junto al mono danzante,
escribiendo en el espejo del alba mensajes
sobre el tiempo por venir, y el búho lunar,
emperchado en el brazo de la muerte

a la orilla de un río acechó el caimán,
con bandas celestes sobre el lomo,
corrió el jaguar de dientes encarnizados
tras el venado en fuga, el águila de alas
traslúcidas en vuelo vislumbró el horizonte
y todo fue un sueño de plumajes verdes y amarillos

HOMERO ARIDJIS

The Creation of the World by the Animals

(according to the *Popol Vuh*)

English version by Kathleen Jamie,
based on a literal translation from the Spanish by Anne McLean

Across an empty darkness,
across unmoving sky,
flashed scarlet macaw –
so day broke: and yellow orioles
with turquoise eyes
began dancing a solo of light

and within a mighty ceiba tree,
the 'mother of birds', appeared
a skinny spider monkey
his privates dangling – and howler-monkey,
scriving prophesies on the mirror of dawn,
and lunar owl, perched on death's arm.

Caiman lurked on a river bank,
his back marked with celestial stripes,
and sharp-fanged jaguar
pursued the fleeing deer; and eagle,
aloft on clear wings, spied the horizon –
and all was a feathered dream: yellow and green.

entonces el cuerpo del hombre
y el cuerpo de la mujer fueron
formados de barro y agua y de madera,
hijos del bosque, del sol y la montaña,
tuvieron ojos para mirarse a sí mismos
y voz para nombrar a los animales

El Corazón del Cielo el Corazón de la Tierra
y el Corazón del Mar fueron una misma cosa
y todas las criaturas de la tierra del agua
y del aire pudieron llevar una sombra
respirar, ser y amar.
Y la creación se hace cada día.

then figured from water, clay and wood,
came woman and man:
offspring of the sun,
children of forest and mountain,
with their eyes they could behold themselves,
their voices named the animals.

Heart of the Sky, Heart of the Sea
Heart of the Earth beat as one,
and all the winged creatures, creatures
of the waters and the land
could be, breathe, love and cast shade.
And life is re-created every day.

رضا محمدی

دود به دود

۱

پشت کسی می‌گردم
که روزی در پیرهنم می‌سوخت
لب به لب
پشت صدایی می‌گردم
که روزی در نخ سیگاری آویختمش
ورق به ورق
پشت فالی می‌گردم
که پرندگان و گیاهان و ابرها را رفته بود

الهی این قاصدک برسد به سفره مادرم
برسد به حویلی پدرم
برسد به رودخانه‌ای که ماهیانش روزی سه بار عاشق می‌شوند
سه بار خودکشی می‌کنند

هی!

REZA MOHAMMADI

Smoke

English version by Nick Laird,
based on literal translations from the Persian by the author
and by Narguess Farzad

1

I'm looking for the man who
used to burn inside my shirt.

At the precipice of each lip
I'm trying to find the voice I once
dangled from a cigarette.

At the turn of the card
I am asking after all the revelation
that swept away the birds and plants
the clouds

Lord, carry off this dandelion
to my mother's laden table.
Take it to my father's house.

Take it to the river where the fish
fall in love three times a day
three times a day they kill themselves.

   Hey!

من شش ساله بیشتر نیستم
آمده بودم نان بخرم، این جا چکار می‌کنم؟

هی!

روحم را به انگشت نگاری ببرید
می‌بینید از کوچه شهاب سه جنب نخورده‌ام
می‌بینید فقط آمده بودم نان بخرم
می‌بینید او شش ساله بیشتر نیست

۲

پیش از آنکه پیش من آید
سرش را صبح خورده بود
عینهو شعری چروکیده در من پرت شد

آهای!

این همه باد در پیرهنم جا نمی‌شود

آهای!

I'm six years old
    and came to buy bread.

What am I doing here?

    Hey!

Carry my soul to the palm reader.
Take it to be finger-printed.

You will see I never left the street
that bears the missile's name.

You will see I only came to buy some rolls of bread.

You will see I am – exactly – six years old.

2

Before the next man joined me
the morning finished gorging on
his head
    and like a folding here
        in the poem
the man was thrown and caught
    within me

    Hey!

This much wind can't fit inside my shirt.

    Hey!

این همه ابر در من قرار نمی‌گیرند
تکه‌هایش باز می‌گردند و سرتان را می‌خورند

چرا از این همه خاک خدا، من
دو خودکار تمام شده دستانش
در من قی کردند
دو فندک شکسته پاهایش
در من مشتعل شدند
و قلبش سیگار نیم سوخته‌ای
که رطوبت زده بود
در جیب‌هایش
مژه‌های مادرش، پلک‌های زنش و موهای خواهرش را کرم‌ها بردند

کاش کسی به او گفته بود ماه در لباس‌های جان لوییس جان نمی‌سوزد
و از من چنانکه از سفره مادرش گریخت
کاش می‌دانست خاک لب‌های شاعران را استحاله می‌کند

This much cloud can't be allowed to land.

Shrapnel of the blackened body
      coming back to eat at you, to
snack on you, to feast.

Why should I be the dust of god, kicked up?

I flow like ink from the pens of his fingers.

The broken lighters of his feet
      flicker-flare in mine

but his heart is spent, a wet cigarette,
and in his pockets worms digest
      his mother's lashes,
the eyelids of his wife,
      fistfuls of his sister's hair.

I wish someone had once told him
how the moon will not burn
in John Lewis clothing.

This one runs from me as he ran
from his mother's table,

and I would like to tell him of
the metamorphosis
the earth
causes in the lips of poets,

how it decomposes.

۳

دریا از من گریخته
کبوتران از من پریدند
و ارغوان‌ها را در من خاک گرفت
آرایش چهره تو چطوری بود؟
روسری تو چه رنگی داشت؟
دوده مردی‌ام که لباس پوشیده
قاصدکی را می‌گیرم
آدرسی به یادم نمی‌آید
خاک روی بال شب‌پره می‌غلتد
خاک روی تن شب‌بو می‌پوسد
و من همه چیز
را
از یاد برده‌ام

3

Even the river escaped me.

Even the doves took flight.

The Judas trees inside me

are made up of the debris.

How was your face made up?

What shade was your headscarf?

Black with soot in my black suit

I hold a dandelion in one hand

but remember no address.

Dust descending on a moth's wings,

dust descending on the petals:

I have forgotten everything.

ANTONELLA ANEDDA

Tre Ghazal

GHAZAL DELLE PAROLE

Capite da sole parole che non vi posso mostrare
con voi farei del male.

Non posso continuare. Non voglio più ferire, non voglio lusingare
devo restare nell'amore minimo di un cerchio familiare.

Dunque parole siate buone andate nel silenzio,
abbasserò la voce fino in fondo.

Dalla bocca ora escono sciami di lettere
e animali come nei cartigli medioevali.

L'incontro dei vivi con i morti
dovrebbe servire soltanto a rinunciare.

ANTONELLA ANEDDA

Three Ghazals

English translation from the Italian by Jamie McKendrick

GHAZAL OF THE WORDS

Words, you've grasped on your own I can't utter you
without doing ill or causing harm.

I can't go on. I don't want to wound or flatter
so I stay within the family circle's minimal warmth.

So words be good, be gone into the silence.
I lower my voice so much it can't be heard.

Out of my mouth letters and animals swarm
as in medieval painted parchments.

The meeting of the quick and the dead
serves only to teach us to renounce.

GHAZAL DEL TUMULARE

'Se ti attardi nel mondo, tutto si dilegua come un sogno'
GOETHE

Verbo dell'osservare: l'acqua che sgorga dalle pietre e poi scompare.
Verbo del rinunciare: la erre si arrota inutilmente e poi scompare.

Il ruotare su un punto della mente coincide con il rifiuto di enunciare.
L'acqua si richiude sul mare, è la lezione del non accumulare.

Un passo dietro l'altro, lo sguardo sui rovi e sui licheni, sui resti delle
ossa
di animale, nulla da conservare. La terra è curva, le stelle si piegano
sui monti.

Ci siamo incontrati amico mio in un minimo segmento orizzontale
dove da tempo non esisteva nessun verbo da declinare.

BURIAL GHAZAL

'If you linger too long in the world, everything dissipates like a dream.'
GOETHE

Verb of observing: water that gushes from a rock then disappears.
Verb of renouncing: the 'r' rolled in vain that disappears.

Circling a point in the mind coincides
with the refusal to pronounce or proclaim.

Water sealed like a lid upon the sea
teaches the futility of hoarding.

One step after another, gaze fixed on thorns
and lichens, on the scattered bones of animals.

Nothing to be preserved. Earth's curve.
Stars lean over the mountains.

We met, my friend, in the narrowest horizontal segment
where for some time there's been no verb to conjugate.

GHAZAL DELLO SCHELETRO

Dice un proverbio che al diavolo non interessano le ossa
forse perché gli scheletri danno una grande pace,

composti nelle teche o in grandi scenari di deserto,
amo il loro sorriso fatto solo di denti, il cranio calvo

la perfezione delle orbite, la mancanza di naso,
il vuoto intorno al sesso e finalmente i peli,

questi orpelli, volati dentro il nulla. Non è un gusto del macabro,
ma il realismo glabro dell'anatomia

lode dell'esattezza e del nitore. Pensarci senza pelle
rende buoni. E per il paradiso

forse non c'è strada migliore
che ritornare pietre, saperci senza cuore.

SKELETON GHAZAL

According to one proverb the devil takes no interest in bones
perhaps because skeletons radiate such peace,

laid in display cases or in wide desert vistas.
I love their smiles composed entirely of teeth, the bald cranium,

those finely rounded sockets, the absence of a nose,
the gap around the sex and finally the hair,

that tinsel, blown away to nothing. It's not a taste
for the macabre but for the stark realism of anatomy,

for neat exactitude. To think of ourselves
shorn of skin ought to make us good-natured.

And is there better way to enter heaven
than to return to stone, to know we have no heart?

أمجد ناصر

أحصنة حديدية

(إلى الأب باولو دالوليو)

قلْ لي ماذا تفعل هنا أيها الغصنُ المنحني؟
كيف وصلت بين الأكفان البيض وأشجار الكوبالت
إلى مآدب الضباع؟
هناك عيون تراك ولا تراها
تنقل الصورة السالبة لشكل الركعة
وترسلها إلى طوطم التمر.
الله
الذي عبدناه طويلاً تخلى عنا في هذا الليل / التيه
ولم نعد نرى له أثراً في سماء النجيع.
الساعات هنا تتوقف عن العمل
والقلب عن القصيدة الطويلة التي ضخ فيها دماً كثيراً.
إذهبْ مثلنا في التيه
إدخلْ في هذا الليل الأرقط،
فلن تصادفَ في الأرجاء،
آلهةً ولا أبطالاً مثلما في الملاحم
وحكاياتِ ما قبل النوم،
فلم تعدْ هذه الصحراء،
التي جئتها بيدين مرفوعتين
تنجبُ أنبياء،
لقد أفرطتْ في ذلك من دون أن يستطيع هؤلاء
انتزاع الوحش الكامن خلف القفص الصدريِّ لأبناء آدم.
اسمح لي، إذن، أن أقول لك:
لا الملائكة ولا الشياطين
بقادرين على وقف نواعير الدم
التي تديرها أرواحٌ شريرةٌ من مكانٍ مجهولٍ،
فلا تفكِّر،

AMJAD NASSER

Iron Horses

English translation from the Arabic by Fady Joudah

(For Paolo Dall'Oglio)

Bent branch, tell me what are you doing here?
How did you manage, through white shrouds and cobalt trees,
to reach the hyenas' feasts?
You don't see the eyes that see you,
that transmit the negative image of bowing with bent knees
to the totem of dates.
The God we've worshipped for so long has abandoned us
in this night, this wandering, we no longer
recognise his trace in the sanguineous heaven.
Here the clock stops.
The heart halts the poem in which it had pumped too much.
Enter the wandering as we have.
Enter this mottled night.
You won't encounter deities or heroes
as in epics or bedtime stories.
This desert, to which you came
with two raised palms like an absurd hope,
no longer begets prophets,
it did plenty of that and none could rip out
the beast crouching behind the human rib cage.
Allow me, then, these redundant words:
no angel or devil
can put an end to this haemophilia
that evil spirits administer from somewhere unknown,
so, think less
of the *Iliad*

بإلياذة هوميروس
بل بجحيم دانتي
غير أنك لن تحتاج فيرجيلو
ليصحبكَ في رحلةٍ بين الأشلاء والأنين،
فأيُّ رَجُلٍ بساقٍ خشبيّةٍ
أو طفلٍ بيده رغيفُ خبزٍ جافٌّ
وعلى خصره مسدسٌ بلاستيكيٌّ،
يستطيع الطواف بك في دوائر الجحيم التسع
لكنك لن ترى طغاةً ومرابينَ
أو مبدّديْ أرواحٍ وجَدَتْ نَفْسَها خطأً في مرمى النيران،
بل وجوهاً امَّحتْ ملامحها،
وأجساداً فقدت أطرافها
وأشجاراً تلتهما النيران لكنها لا تحترق.

قد تفكّرُ أنك في الآخرة،
وهذا خطأٌ
فأنت لا تزال في الحياة الدنيا
ولكن تشابهتْ عليك الصور،
سترى سماءً خفيضةً
تتساقطُ منها البراميلُ بدل الأمطار
فلا ماء لهذه الأرض المُشقَّقة من العطش.
أنظرْ،
الأحصنةُ الحديديةُ تعبُّ الدمَ
بصرف النظر عن فصيلته
فمن يهمه، هنا، مثل هذه التفاصيل.
عَطَشٌ.
هناك أنهارٌ من الدم
بيد أنها لا تروي.
دمٌّ وملحٌ.
دمٌّ وبلازما.
دمٌّ.
دمٌّ.

and more of Dante's *Inferno*,
though you won't need Virgil to accompany you
through body parts and moaning.
Any man with a wooden leg
or a child holding a stale loaf of bread
with a plastic gun holstered to his waist
can parade you around the nine circles of Hell.
But you won't find tyrants and loan sharks
or soul annihilators snuffed by chance in the line of fire.
Instead, you'll come across faceless faces
and limbless corpses
and trees that fire devours but doesn't burn.

You might think you've arrived at Judgement Day.
You'd be wrong.
You're still in this earthly life,
though images sometimes confound.
You'll notice a low-lying sky
from which barrels, not rain, fall,
for this parched earth gets no water.
Look,
iron horses gulp blood
irrespective of its type,
who cares about such details.
Thirst.
And there are rivers of blood
that don't quench.
Blood and salt.
Plasma.
Blood
and blood.

This earth is like a stray dog that got a kick in its side from a military boot
and started yowling, yelping into the solitary, symphonic echo of pain.

هذه الأرض مثل كلبٍ شاردٍ تلقَّى ركلةً على خاصرته من بسطارٍ فراحت تعوي وتعوي
ولا شيء يرتدُّ إلا الصدى السيمفوني للآلام.
لا تحتاج درويشاً يدور إلى الأبد،
حول الشكل الهندسيّ الأمثل للنقطة
كي يقول إنَّ مَنْ يشربُ الدمَ يزدادُ عطشاً،
ولا قديساً،
أو أفّاقاً بلحيةٍ شيباء،
يصرخ في الجموع التي تتقافز
من طبقة في الجحيم الى أخرى:
اغفروا لاعدائكم.

* * *

صوت من الصحراء:

أنا نبيٌ من دون ديانة ولا أتباع. نبيٌ نفسي. لا ألزمُ أحداً بدعوتي ولا حتى أنا،
إذ يحدثُ أن أكفر بنفسي، وأجدِّفَ على رسالتي. نبي ماذا؟ ومَنْ؟ لا أعرف شيئاً
في هذه الظلمة التي تلفّني. لا أحمل صليباً على ظهري وليس لي عصا تشقُّ البحر.
أتلمَّس طريقي بالضوء الصادر من عينيٌ ولا أرى يدي التي تلوّح لجموعٍ وهميةٍ
تموج تحت سفح الجبل.

* * *

أخطو فأخطو في هذا الليل/التيه
كمن يتوقعُ أيَّ شيء من قلب الانسان/
صدري مفعم ٌبخضرةٍ/
لا بدّ أن هناك من يخطو مثلي في أمكنةٍ أخرى/
لست وحيداً في هذا الليل الجامع/
بقدميَّ الملفوفتين بخرقة الأولياء القدامى
أدوسُ الرمل،
الحجر/
العوسج/
الذهب الخام/
التراب المرتاب/

It doesn't need a dervish spinning eternally around an invisible point
to say that whoever drinks blood grows thirstier.

And no saint
or a hobo with grey beard
to scream at the crowds that leap
from one rank of Hell to another:
Forgive your enemies.

* * *

A voice from the desert:

I am a prophet without religion or follower, prophet of myself, I impose
my invitation on no one, not even me, as I sometimes disbelieve in
myself and curse my message. What prophet? And whose? I know
nothing about this darkness that wraps me in it. I feel my way with
the light my eyes emit but I don't see my hand as it waves to imaginary
masses who wave below the mountain.

* * *

I step into this night/ this wandering as someone who puts nothing
past a human heart/ my chest infused with evergreen/ there must be
another person who sets foot in other places as I do/ I'm not alone in
this universal night/ on my feet that are wrapped with the rags of ear-
ly guardians/ not alone as I step on sand, stone, boxthorn/ pure gold/
distrustful dust/ for who knows what one treads on in total darkness/
blindness isn't an eye disease but a weakness of heart muscle/ I step into
this night while holding a guidebook for the perplexed/ I hear someone
say 'Come in, sit with us under this stray star/ the road is longer than
three days that three wells separate, and on each well three crows/ a
mustard seed in the beak of the first, a wheat grain in the second, and
in the third a pearl.'

فمن يعرفُ أيَّ شيء يدوسُ المرءُ في الليل التامّ/
العمى ليس مرضاً في العينين
بل ضعفٌ في عضلة القلب/
أخطو الى هذا الليل وفي يدي دليل الحائرين/
أسمعُ من يقول: تفضّل اجلس معنا تحت هذه النجمة الضّالة/ لِمَ العجلة/ الحيُّ يؤنس الميت/ والطريق أطول من ثلاثة نهاراتٍ تفصل بينها ثلاثُ آبارٍ عليها ثلاثةُ غربانٍ في منقار الأول حبّةُ خردلٍ، وفي منقار الثاني حبّةُ قمحٍ، وفي منقار الثالث لؤلؤةٌ

* * *

ليس للضوء أكثر من اسم في لغتك المتوسطية،
لكن على الجانب الآخر من هذا الليل / التيه
حيث يتكاثرُ القتلةُ في وضح النهار،
اسم نطقته بعربيةٍ سوريّةٍ فصحى:
النّور.
ففي أيِّ ظلمةٍ،
أو نورٍ داخليٍّ،
ترزحُ،
الآنَ،
أيها الرجلُ الذي حملَ قلبَه على كفّه وصعدَ به الى جبلٍ بلا عشبةٍ أو قطرة ماء،
وزرعه هناك فأثمر شجرةً ترخي ظلالها لأيِّ عابر سبيلٍ تحت شمسٍ تشتغلُ، أحياناً، جلاداً في الظهيرات.
أشكُّ أنك تعرفُ أنَّ الحبَّ يخيفُ إلى هذا الحدّ، وأنَّ في الكلمة سرّاً لا يفهمُ خطورتَه إلا الأشرار،
كان ينبغي أن تحيا كأنك ميتٌ،
أو تموتَ مثلنا كأنك حيٌّ
لتذكّرَ بالجرائم التي لن يُحاسبَ عليها أحدٌ من فرط كثرتها.
قل أين أنتَ لآتيك بالقلم والقرطاس،
بالإبرةِ والخيطِ،
بالخبز والزيت،
بشربة ماء تقطّرت
من أعين الممدَّدين على الأرض
ينتظرون المجارف والأكفان.

* * *

In your Mediterranean language, light
has only one name.
But on the other side of this night, this labyrinth
where killers proliferate in daylight,
there's a name you pronounced
in perfect Syrian Arabic:
'Noor.'
Tell me,
in which darkness
or inner light
do you now
decay?
Man, with his heart in his palm, man who climbed with it up a water-
less grassless mountain then planted his heart where a tree sprouted
to loosen its shadows over any visitor caught in a sun that sometimes
works as hangman at noon: I doubt you know that love can be this
frightening, and that in words there are secrets whose danger only the
evil comprehend. You should have lived as if you were dead or should
have died as we do: fully alive, to recall the crimes that will go unac-
counted for, for they are countless.
Tell me where you are now,
and I will bring you pen and paper,
thread and needle,
bread and oil,
a drop of water
from the eyes of those who, supine on the ground,
wait for shovel and shroud.

DON PATERSON

Eleven Maxims from the Book of Ill-Humour

I
Read a poem slow enough
With vigilance and care
And you'll discover lots of stuff
that simply isn't there

II
In the country of the two-eyed, it's the same:
The one-eye'd man still has the better aim.

III
On his deathbed, much too late, a voice came from afar
And sang that line he'd once heard in a film, or in a bar:
No one will ever love you for everything you are

IV
And then did God make man and woman – bless! –
For company. Ironic, wouldn't you say:
Someone might have told him neediness
Is no one's most attractive quality.

V
As a trumpet's how you toot it
an idea's how you put it

VI
A *poet* for a friend?
As far as they're concerned
all you represent's

an inconvenience
standing in the way
of a decent elegy

VII
Even in Kyoto, as he said in his haiku,
Bashō was still longing for Kyoto.
But I don't suppose that Bashō really could've had a clue
that *all* of us are longing for Kyoto.

VIII
Poets: if it already *has* a name,
stop bothering it.

IX
Don't forget her, son,
heartbroken as you are;
it's a waste of a good wound
to heal without a scar.

X
As mass structures space
So death structures time;
Gently, from afar;
But were you to alight
And try to stand upright
Upon its cratered face
You could not tell apart
The ticking and the chime.

XI
The poet takes his pen
And settles down to write
in the fullness of the dawn
like it's the dead of night.

فاطمه شمس

نوار قلب

پشتم تیر می‌کشد
سه ماه پیش قلبم را جابه‌جا کردند
گذاشتند در ستون فقراتم
کنار مهره سیزدهم
حالا زندگی‌ام بسته به رگ باریکیست که خون را از آن حفره تاریک خالی
به قلب جدیدم می‌ریزد
رگ زبان‌نفهم کبود!
قلب پتیاره‌ی هرجایی!
این روزها اخبار را از نوار قلبم می‌گیرم
سرخط خبرها به گذشته مربوط است
به زنی که می‌خندید
به مردی که عاشقش بودم
به تلفن‌های شنود
و قلب‌های سالم سرشار.
قلب، پنجره‌ایست
رو به غربت‌های پی‌درپی
این حجم ماهیچه‌ای سرخ
کاش آینه‌ای بود رو به اکنون.

تیم پزشکی با لبخندی دوستانه: «کمی جابه جایی لازم بود
ساعتت را از امروز با قلبت تنظیم کن!»
ساعت‌های شماته‌دار پوسیده...
معشوق تازه‌ام دیشب پرسید: «فکر می کنی تحت نظر هستیم؟»
فکر کردم دارد درصد جنون و توهمم را محک می‌زند
سایه‌های سمج را از او پنهان کردم
چشم‌های سایه‌ها را تمام این سال‌ها

FATEMEH SHAMS

Electrocardiogram

English translation from the Persian by Dick Davis

My back aches
Three months ago they moved my heart
They put it in my spine
Next to the thirteenth vertebra
Now my life depends on a thin vein that empties blood from that dark
    pit into my new heart
My idiotic bruise of a vein!
My wanton whore of a heart!
These days I get my news from my ECG
The headlines are about the past
About a woman who used to laugh
About a man I loved once
About tapped telephones
And lavishly healthy hearts.
The heart is a window
Facing one exile after another
This bunched red muscle
I wish it were a mirror, facing Now.

The medical team, with a friendly smile: 'We had to move it a bit;
From today on, set your watch by your heart!'
The rotted alarm clocks . . .
Last night my new lover asked, 'Do you think we're being watched?'
I thought he was quizzing me to see how crazy and paranoid I am
I hid my willful shadows from him
For years I've hidden my shadows' eyes in my dresses

در پیراهن‌هایم پنهان کرده بودم
از شهری به شهر دیگر
سایه آخر قلبی خون‌آلود را در مشت گرفته بود و می‌دوید.
پزشکان با سایه‌ها دشمنند
و در تشخیص پارانویا حاذق.
آن‌ها خوب می‌دانند چطور برای تبعید نسخه بپیچند:
جابه‌جایی قلب
در روزگاری که جای هیچ زخمی با هیچ قلبی
خوب نمی‌شود.

From one city to another
The last shadow was running with a bloody heart in his fist.
Doctors are the enemies of shadows
And experts in diagnosing paranoia.
They know very well what to prescribe for exile:
Moving the heart
In times when no scar of any heart
Will heal.

GILLES ORTLIEB

Mind the Gap

Après les montagnes d'Albanie aperçues à travers le hublot, aussi duveteuses
et spongieuses que des bouillons de culture dans l'oculaire d'un microscope,
et les flaques de mercure de lacs au loin, voici les montagnes de Grèce enfin
et ses bords dentelés, avant que la carlingue ne se pose sur le tarmac de juillet
comme on ouvrirait la porte d'un four. Retour au pays où les citrons fleurissent
et qui marche sur un tapis crissant de cigales tandis que l'Hymette, à la crête
hérissée d'antennes – ou de banderilles – s'apprête à s'assombrir dans le soir
tombant jusqu'à coincider avec la teinte d'une figue mûre. Les cris des gosses
montant d'un jardin public : un pépiement d'ombres parmi les fûts de colonnes
du *logos* antique, voix de jadis et d'aujourd'hui s'appelant dans la cité sinistrée.
Platon négocie désormais des véhicules d'occasion, Euripide derrière son bar
sert des cafés glacés à emporter, le marbre du Pentélique bordure les trottoirs
et les méandres de l'Ilissos asséché, disparu dans l'herbe et sous les voitures,
ornementent des plaques d'égout. Il suffit encore pourtant, dit-on, d'un oignon
pour dresser une table, le plus important restant de savoir avec qui la partager :
le dénuement se charge d'enseigner l'art et les manières. *Mind the gap*, ai-je lu
dans le train vers Le Pirée, entre la rame et le quai, entre l'autre et soi, l'Orient
et l'Occident, le grec d'Homère ou de Sappho et celui des apostrophes alentour.
Deux oreilles et deux yeux pour une seule bouche, il s'agira moins de parler ici
que de voir, d'écouter et, comme Goethe s'isolant des canonnades de l'Empire

GILLES ORTLIEB

Mind the Gap

English version by Sean O'Brien,
based on a literal translation from the French by Frank Wynne

After a glimpse of the mountains of Albania from the porthole,
downy and yielding like cultures in the gaze of the microscope,
after the distant lakes of mercury, here at last are the peaks
and ragged shores of Greece, and no sooner has the plane touched down
on the melted tarmac of July than the heat is there
in the open door of the furnace. A return to the country where
lemon trees blossom, the country that moves like a rustling
mat of cicadas, while in the gathering dusk Hymettus – its crest
bristling with antennae like banderillas – prepares itself for night
by assuming the shade of a ripened fig. And the shouts of kids rising
from the public gardens; the discourse of chirruping shadows
among the columns of ancient *logos*; voices past and present
calling to each other across the ruined city. Nowadays Plato deals
in used cars, and the barista Euripides sells takeaway frappé;
the marble of Mount Petelicus edges the pavements, the meanders
of Ilyssos run dry, vanished or embossed on manhole covers.
And yet, they say, an onion is still enough to lay a table: what matters
is to know who ought to share it, for the task of destitution is to teach
both art and courtesy. *Mind the gap*, I read, on the train to Piraeus,
between the platforms and the train, between self and other, East and West,
the Greek of Homer or of Sappho and the street-cries everywhere.
This is a matter less of speech than of listening and looking, and –
like Goethe taking shelter from the cannonade at Valmy, or Gautier

ou Théophile Gautier ignorant la tempête contre ses vitres fermées, de chercher refuge et patrie dans cette langue apprise, ânonnée sur les marchés et psalmodiée dans les églises – alphabet résonnant dans un puits sans fond. Qui ne se contente de peu (mais ce peu-là est, ici, millénaire) ne pourra jamais se satisfaire de rien.

tuning out the thunder at his window – seeking out a refuge and a home
inside this language, whether learnèd, or stammered in the agora,
or chanted in a church – an alphabet that echoes in a well
no one has fathomed. Whoever cannot be content with little
(and a little here is a millenium) can be content with nothing.

مريد البرغوثي

طاعةُ الماءْ

كم سهراً وكم مهارة وكم تخصصاً وكم ترددا وتضحية
تحتاجُ إن أردتَ صُنعَ آلةٍ رخيصةٍ أو غالية؟
وكل ما تحتاجه لصنع طاغية
أن تنحني

* * *

لا، ليس خرتيتاً وليس معجزة
بل ربما يشبهني ويشبهكْ
وهذه ليست كما حسبتَها، أظلافَهُ
بل إنها أظافرٌ عاديةٌ، كأنها أظافري، كأنها أظافرك،
نعم. وليست هذه حوافره
بل إنها حذاؤه، نمرته ثمانيةٌ،
أو تِسعةٌ كما أظُنْ
نعم. ووَزنُ جسمِهِ، ليس كما تراهُ، نصفَ طنْ،
بل مثلنا، سبعون، قُلْ تسعينَ، كيلوغرامْ
وليس هذا قرنَهُ، بل أنْفُهُ المرفوعُ واثقاً، حتى وإن أصابه الزكامْ
نعم. وإنه يصيبه الزكامْ
نعم. وقد يُصيبهُ، كما يصيبكَ، النزيفْ.

* * *

MOURID BARGHOUTI

The Obedience of Water

English version by George Szirtes,
based on a literal translation from the Arabic by Khaled Aljbailli

How many nights of art, close study, hesitation and sacrifice,
at little or great expense, do you need to invent
the simplest of gadgets?
All you need to invent a tyrant is a single
bend of the knee.

* * *

No, he's not a rhino, not a miracle,
in fact he may look like you. Or me.
Don't be fooled. Those are not his claws
they are perfectly normal nails like yours.
Nor are those hooves, no,
they are his size eight, possibly
size nine, shoes.
He's less heavy than you think. No, not a ton,
just the weight of an ordinary man,
say seventy or eighty kilos.
Is that his horn? No
it's his smug little, snub little nose and, yes,
he might catch a cold like you and I.
He might even bleed.

* * *

هو لا يأتي من أكتاف الغيمات إلى كرسيه
بل من أكتافك أنت وأكتافي
ويُدَلِّي رجليهِ على سرج الوقتْ،
وأؤكد أن له رجلينِ فقط لا سِتٌّ
يهوَى المِرآةَ وتهوى أن تهواه ويهواها

ويحب القانون فلا يقتل نَفْساً، أو يهدم بيتاً أو يذبح بضعة آلاف إلا بالقانون
وفي عهده
تبدو الآمال إهانات لذكاء الناس فتومض كي تخبو
وتعود تضيء بلا سبب معروف

* * *

يترجم ارتعاشَهُ صلابةً مهما جرى
لأنه يريد منا أن نكون ماءٌ
آراؤنا رأي الإناءْ
يريد أن يرى ركودنا المقيم دائماً في قاع كوب
وننحني إذا انحنى الإبريق في يده
ونحبس الكلام في الحلوق
لكننا حين انتوينا، كلُّنا، ما ينتويه الماء
عَلَتْ يداهُ باستغاثةٍ أخيرةٍ ... واستغربَ الغرقْ

When he takes his seat he doesn't descend from heaven
on a cloud, no, he climbs up on our shoulders, yours and mine
and sits in the saddle of time dangling his legs,
two legs not six, if you care to check.
His mirror loves him. He loves his mirror. The love is mutual.

He adores the law. Any house he burns, anyone he kills,
any massacre he orders, is done in full accordance with the law.
Don't insult your own intelligence
by hoping. Let that flame flicker, die, and unaccountably flicker again
while he's in charge.

* * *

He regards even his tantrums as a sign of strength.
He would prefer us to be as water,
to see us stagnating at the bottom of the cup.
We must bow when he pours us out,
Not allowing a word to escape
and yet when we behaved like water as he intended
he raised his hands in mute appeal, astonished to be drowning.

JAAN KAPLINSKI

Великий топор

Все знали, что с детства он мечтал стать топором,
бороться с врагами, рубить головы и лес.
Он вырос и рубил. Щепки летели, головы падали.
Все должны были верить: он самый самый острый,
самый безжалостный из всех топоров, он выкован из самый
    твердой
нержавеющей стали. Но никто не должен был знать,
что он обыкновенный железный топор.
Он боялся ржавчины. Стоя один перед зеркалом,
он проверял, нет ли на его лезвии
новых красноватых пятен. Он пытался смыть,
скрыть ржавые пятна пятнами свежей крови.
Но ржавчины становилось больше, кровь не смогла ее смыть.
Пока однажды, упавши сквозь зеркало, что он в ярости разбил,
он попал на другую сторону, в зазеркалье,
на опушку леса недалеко от большого болота. И он понял,
что его место там, в болотном озерце, где он потихоньку
снова станет комком темно-бурой болотной руды.

JAAN KAPLINSKI

The Great Axe

English translation from the Russian by Sasha Dugdale

Everyone knew that from childhood he had dreamed of becoming an axe
to fight his enemies, to chop off heads and branches.
He grew up and chopped – and splinters flew, heads fell
and everyone had to believe: that he was sharpest of all
the most pitiless of all axes, cast from the toughest steel
that would never rust. But no one must ever know that
he was a normal iron axe.
He was afraid of rust. Standing alone before the mirror
he would check, were those new reddish stains
on his blade? He tried to wash them away
to cover the rust stains with the stain of fresh blood
but the rust grew, the blood could not cover it.
Until one day, he smashed the mirror in anger, fell through it,
and found himself on the other side of the looking-glass
on the edge of a forest near a large swamp. And realised
that his place was there, in the swamp's pool, where he
could be transformed back into a fist of mud-brown bog ore.

نجوم الغانم

الظِّلال القُرْمُزيّة

ح

وإنْ سرَقَتْ فينوس مِنّا مَواعيدَنا؛ وعبَثَ المشتريْ بطَوالِعنا
فلن ندَعَهُما يُنشدانِ افتراقَ دُروبِنا.
سنترُكُ لِلأقدارِ وردةَ الأُمْنياتِ
لَرُبّما خانَ السَّدنةُ الأعرافَ مِن أجلِنا رَيثما
نصعَدُ إلى اللهِ الذي سيَمْنحُنا باباً ومفْتاحَ نجاةٍ
ويَغفِرُ لنا لأنّنا نُريدُ أنْ نَهبِطَ مِن جنّتِه.
رُبّما لا بَأسَ إنْ سقطْنا مرّةً.

ز

رحلْتَ مُقْتَفياً مَزاميرَ هِليوس
غَسلْتَ الطُّرُقاتِ بالمِلحِ لِئلا يبقى مِن رائِحتِنا
شيءٌ عالِقٌ في الحَجر.
بَكيْتُ عليكَ حتى اخترَقَ قلبي بجُرْحِ الغِيابِ
ورغمَ سَطوةِ الحُزنِ خبّأْتُ لعَودتِك قوافيَ «حافظ»
وظِلِّ الأنْجُمِ القُرْمُزيّةِ،
تركْتُ النوافِذَ مُشرعةً تحْتَ سماءِ أيْلول،
وحينَ لم تأتِ تعلّمْتُ مُناداةَ الرّيح.
عشِقْتُ الحُبَّ في الانتظارِ
وكان لَسْعُ الثّلجِ الحارِقُ على وَجنَتيَّ يَشْفي قلبي.

NUJOOM ALGHANEM

The Crimson Shades

English version by Doireann Ní Ghríofa
based on a literal translation from the Arabic by Suneela Mubayi

'H'

If, in thievery, Venus should steal those who were our destiny;
    if Jupiter draws mischief on us furtively,
Should these odds come to pass, we will not permit their rude
    attempts to split our paths;
No. Upon those fates we will bestow the rose of hope,
For who is to say that the shrines' custodians may not, for our sake,
    choose to betray the old ways,
While we soar to god, who will gift us not only a door and a key of
    redemption,
but also give his forgiveness, should we wish our descent again from
    heaven.
Perhaps this single fall will be permissible?

'S'

You voyaged following Helios's Psalms.
No scent of us remained on the stones
once your salt had scrubbed the paths.
I wept until the gashes of absence charred my heart.
Despite my overwhelming grief, I concealed the verses of Hafiz
in the crimson shades of stars.
Under September skies, I threw windows wide.

البدرُ الّذي أَمرَضَهُ شَوقي أصبحَ بَيتاً أَلوذُ إليه،
والمفازاتُ أرضُ أَحْلامي،
أمّا مَضائقُ البُلدانِ فكانَتِ الْجِسرَ الذي سأعبُرُهُ لأصِلَ إلى قلبِكَ.
كُنّا سنفْتَحُ قُمصانَ المساءاتِ ونَتَداوى بالقُبْلاتِ
لكنَّك أَخذْتَ الأناشيدَ مِن يدَيْها وبقيتَ هُناكَ في
البُحورِ «الطَّويلةِ» تَخْتبرُ وَقْعَ أوزانِها وتُقلّبُ المَوجَ...

رحلْتَ في الرّحيلِ
وصار قَدَرُ العِشقِ بينَنا هو الفِراقُ.

ح

تَعالَيْ لِلَيلةِ اكْتِمالِ القمرِ
نَفترِشُ في ظِلهِ جزيرَتَنا ونَتّكِئُ على رِياح الجَنوب
ستَدوخُ أقْدارُنا مِن شِدّةِ عِشقِنا وتَمنحُنا ساعةً أو اثنَتَيْنِ،
نَتذوّقُ في غَفلتِها القُبْلَةَ فوقَ القُبلةِ...
وربّما نَسِيَتْنا حيثُما نحنُ لألفِ ليلةٍ وليلةٍ أُخرى...
هكذا كَقُبْلةِ الغَيْمةِ للغَيمةِ
نَشتعِلُ كُلّما اقْتربَتْ أرواحُنا ويَنْهمِرُ المطرُ على العالَمِ
كالقُبْلةِ فوقَ القُبْلةِ.

When you still didn't arrive, I turned to the winds and cried,
Oh, and as I waited, I fell in love with love.
I willed snow's cheek-scorch to heal my heart.
Now I make my home in the full moon, infected as it is by my
    desire-pangs,
and my dreams rest in desert clefts.
The sand-bridges which lead to distant lands always carried me to
    your warm heart
When we longed to unbutton evening's blouse and clothe each other
    in kisses from our red mouths,
Until you filched the hymns from their grip and chose to rest instead
in the ocean's lyric depths, testing each metric constriction, flicking
    through ripples.

Within the flight you flew away, within the crossing, you crossed,
    astray,
until you turned your face away, and our love was destined to division
    and disarray.

'H'

Return for a night as the moon turns full,
and you and I will lie on our island in shadows of moon-gloom.
    We'll lean in southerlies,
Our desires so strong that even our fates will spin dizzy, allowing us
    secret hours
To sip kiss over kiss.
Our mouths will mimic the embrace of clouds –
The closer our souls, the more rain rushes down
each droplet a kiss falling into a kiss.

ز

نَرْشو الْجِنِّيَاتِ لِتُهرِّبَنا كوَزْنٍ في قصيدةٍ إذنْ؟   فتَكْتفي هيَ
بحكايةٍ لنا في كِتابِها   ونَكتفي نحنُ بالقُبَلِ فوقَ القُبَلِ؟
أيَّ رِيحٍ نَرْشو؟   أشرْقيَّةٌ أم غربيّةٌ تلك التي ستختارنا؟

ح

بل رُبَّما شَماليّةٌ أو كِيمياءُ يُبْدِعُها اللهُ لنا
لنَسقُطَ أوَّلاً في الليلِ كالنَّجمةِ خلفَ النَّجمةِ
ثُم نكونَ رَمادَها وسِرَّ أسْرارِها؟
فالعشقُ مَوتٌ مُحتملٌ   وما أحْلاهُ   إنْ كان لنا فيه نَصيبٌ.

'S'

Might we bribe the fire-jinns to hide us in a poem, like metre or
    rhythm? Might our myth,
if written in the book, be to their satisfaction? Might we allow
    ourselves contentment
to sip kisses on kisses? Which wind might we bribe? Which breeze
    will conceal us:
the easterly, or the westerly?

'H'

Maybe the north wind or some secret chemistry created for us by God
Will permit us to plummet first into the darkness, as star after star falls
    forth from the night sky,
that we might be their ashes and their secret of secrets
for falling in love is a probable death, yet how beautiful it would be if
    that were to become our destiny.

RAOUL SCHROTT

suleika spricht

woher ich komme? ist wieder und wieder die frage
mir ist der weg kaum mehr recht bewusst
sie trifft auch meinen vater – mit derselben anklage
deretwegen er gehen musste um den verlust
von familie und land hier gutzumachen als taxifahrer
und mit zwei gläsern billigen weins sobald die schicht endet
er sieht sich nunmehr als bewahrer
unseres glaubens und hebt shiraz in den himmel als wäre es das paradies
vergessen die missgunst von seines gottes stellvertretern samt ihrer alibis
erst mit 15 habe ich meine augen vor ihm nicht mehr zu boden gewendet
und bin doch seitdem in geiselhaft
der dünkleren haut der schwarzen haare und der nase wegen
die kein hidjab aus der welt schafft
das tuch trotzdem nicht abzulegen
heiss jetzt frau zu werden bar aller abschätzigen blicke von aussen
um darunter das zu sein was man ist
ein leben ist nur zu führen wenn man sich nicht selbst vermisst
aber das ist leicht gesagt in diesem frankenhausen
und schwer getan · ich durfte dolmetsch studieren
und stosse dabei allerorts auf worte die eine kehrseite besitzen
sodass sie am ende ihre bedeutung verlieren:
weg und weg · pass und pass · schloss und schloss · bank und bank
welche seite vereinahmt mich? diese seite?
beiden gemein ist das unbefreite
arm und der arm mit den ungeübten notizen

RAOUL SCHROTT

suleika speaks

English version by Paul Farley,
based on a literal translation from the German by Shaun Whiteside

where are you from? time and again the same question
I'm barely aware of the journey and route
my father gets it too – with the same accusation
that forced him to leave and make amends
for the loss of family and land as a cabbie here – he salutes
with two glasses of plonk as soon as his shift ends
and sees himself now as the keeper
of our faith and raises Shiraz skywards like it's paradise
forgotten the resentment of his god's reps along with their alibis
I stared at the floor when he was around until
I was fifteen and have been held hostage since with my deeper
skin and darker hair and the nose
which no hijab can remove from the world · still
not taking off the veil has meant
becoming a woman despite the daggers of those
outside: to be what I am beneath · a life can be led
only if you don't miss yourself · easily said
in a sprawling twilit northern settlement
like this but harder to do · allowed to train up
as an interpreter I'm surrounded by words that slip
their definition · that flip and lose their message:
hide and hide · match and match · lock and lock · bank and bank
which side will take me in? on the page
common to both is the hand to mouth
and the hand that makes these awkward notes

in einer sprache die mir nicht mehr fremd ist und dennoch so blank
dass mit ihr alles aufs neue beginnen könnte
so man mir den raum dafür gönnte
mit der deutschen freundschaft hat es keine not –
der ärgerlichsten feindschaft steht höflichkeit zu gebot
keiner beschwere sich über das niederträchtige
was immer man dir auch sagt: es bleibt das mächtige
wie euer goethe meint · wie also weitermachen – auf sich gestellt
gleich einer bettlerin die sich im niemandsland aufhält?
sie und sie · star und star · kiefer und kiefer
feiner regen auf dem entblössten unterarm
die dämmerung gelb · das licht bald tiefer
weshalb vermag zeit soviel hoffnungen zu verheissen wie harm?

in a language no longer strange to me yet so blank
that everything could reboot
if I were allowed enough elbow room
no rush for German hospitality –
politeness serves the worst kind of hostility
no point complaining about spite
whatever they say to you: what remains is might
see Goethe · so how to go on – having to fend
for yourself · like a bag lady wandering the edgelands:
smart and smart · pine and pine · crow and crow
a mizzling rain on the bared forearm
the light lowering · the dusk yellow
how can time promise as many hopes as harms?

محمد بنيس

نشيدُ الفجْر

يا سيّدَ الشّعراءِ غُوتَه
غنّيْتُ من أدْنَى بلادِ الشرقِ كأساً كنتَ تشربُها سعيداً
تحتَ داليةٍ وتعرفُ أنها خيْرٌ تماماً كلُّها

وحدي هُنا في حَانةِ الغُرباءِ يمْلأُ كأسيَ السّاقي
نبيذاً صافياً
كأساً تلي كأساً
وفي سرّي أباركُ نشوةً
مُتنسّكاً أتعلّمُ الغرْبَ الذي أوْدعتَهُ في جوْهرِ الكلماتِ

أنتَ أنا
أراكَ اليوْمَ من زمنٍ إلى زَمنٍ تعودُ
تُطلُّ منْ معْراجِكَ الكوْنيّ يجْمعُ بيْننَا حُلمٌ
تكوّنَ منْ مَدادِكَ عندمَا سُكِرٌ
وشطحٌ فيكَ ظلاّ طائريْنِ إلى الأعَالي شُعلةً يتلألآنْ

حقّاً سأرْفعُ ضوْءَ كأسكَ
لا سبيلَ سواهُ في زمني الجَريحِ كأنما شوقٌ إليْكَ يقودُ
من غرْبٍ إلى شرقٍ يدُورُ الكأسُ لي سُكّرٌ
يُمجّدُ ما يديمُ عليَّ أنْ أحيا بعيداً عن غباءِ الحقْدِ

أعرفُ أن وقتَ الضّيْقِ صارَ اليوْمَ أغْتَى
باسم مَا سمّوْهُ شرْعيةً
ولكنّي بماءِ الحُبّ أغسلُ ما تدنّسَ في النّفوسْ

MOHAMMED BENNIS

Aubade

English version by Sinéad Morrissey,
based on a literal translation from the Arabic by Mbarek Sryfi

O Goethe Master of Poets
from the most Westerly land of the East have I sung in praise
of the glass you raised to happiness under a grapevine
and saw goodness in all things blossom

Alone at the bar, strangers everywhere,
the waiter is filling my glass with wine
glass after glass
and I bless this inner welling bliss
which shows me the West, the West you distilled to its literal essence

You have become me –
Today I see you, flickering revenant,
looking down at me from the whirl of your ascension
the two of us bound by the self-same dream,
together entranced by the spell your ink cast
when waywardness and drunkenness remained steadfast
sparks flying upwards

Yes, I'll raise your light-filled glass
These damaged days, I have no other choice but this
as if my thirst to be one with you could set down a path
from West to East place in my hands the intoxicating glass
carry me far from the stupidity of hate
glorify everything that makes me carry on living

أهْلاً بكأسٍ مِنْ نبيـذٍ يُشبه الياقُوت
سأشربُ في مديح العِشقِ هذا الكأسَ ليْلاً ثم ليْلاً
سوْفَ أسْعَى مُخْلصاً لنشيدِ مِنْ غِنّى
منَ الشعراءِ للأرضِ التي تبقَّى
لنَا أُمّاً كما كانتْ

أنَا السّكرانُ
أبصرُ آيةَ المجهولِ مُشرقةً
على صمْتٍ توحَّدَ بي
وفيّاً لانْفتاح اللانهايةِ بيْننا
فرَحاً به أبداً أكونْ

In this time of hardship, truth bickered over by despots,
with the water of love shall I wash the soul
clean of all profanity

So welcome, glass of ruby-jewelled wine!
From this glass will I drink in praise of love
night after night will I faithfully strive
to praise those amongst the host of poets
who sang for the land – as it once was and ever shall be –
the poets' mother country

I, the drunk –
I see the wondrous unknown shining
on a silence that cocks its head and beckons
In the spaces between us, infinity opens
This my faith, this my happiness

ALEŠ ŠTEGER

Žeja

Vsaka steklenica me uči
Ponižnosti. Če sam Stvarnik
Se pomanjšal je na polič,
Kako neznatna kapljica sem šele jaz?

Srkam njegovo omamno skrivnost.
Skozi usta vstopa vame
In me dela večjega
In bolj zgovornega.

Večji sem, ker je v meni
On, ki je vse.
Vpijem, saj skozme
On vse izreka.

Vsaka, prav vsaka steklenica
Me uči ponižnosti.
Oh, naj se ta sladka šola
Nikoli ne konča.

Če se pa Učitelj moj
Kdaj zadrži ali celo umanjka,
Si Njegove ponižnosti
Z veseljem sam dolijem.

ALEŠ ŠTEGER

Thirst

English translation from the Slovenian by Brian Henry

Every bottle teaches me
Humility. If even the creator
Is reduced by the carafe,
How fine a drop am I?

I sip his intoxicating mystery.
It enters through my mouth
And makes me larger
And more eloquent.

I am larger, because he
Who is everything is in me.
I shout because he is conveying
Everything through me.

Each and every bottle
Teaches me humility.
Oh, let this sweet lesson
Never end.

And if my teacher sometimes restrains
Himself or is missing entirely,
I myself happily refill
His humility.

GONCA ÖZMEN

Bile İsteye

I

Gölgenin verdiği bir cinnet vardı - tattım
Olmadım deyince olunuyor değil

Sevgilim - beni eve götürme geceleri
Beni en çok eve, en çok geceleri

Sandığımı deş, harmanımı yak, yollara düşür
Bendeki taşra geniş odalara alışık değil

Sana bunları hep tek tek
Zemberekten birer birer geçirerek

Sevgilim - beni bağışla geceleri, en çok geceleri
Bırak oyalansın o aç kalabalık dansımda

Gövdem kederden bir tabanca
Üstünde patlayabilmez değil

Götürme beni o apansız kapana
Ev dediğin ne ki kaçtığımın yanında

GONCA ÖZMEN

Knowingly Willingly

English version by Jo Shapcott,
based on a literal translation from the Turkish by Maureen Freely
and Özge Çallı Spike

I

The shadows were so insane I tasted them
And spoke them, though I said I wouldn't

Love, never take me home again
Least of all to that house, and especially not at night

Empty my bottom drawer, incinerate my garden,
Fling me out like the hick I am,

So awkward in your tall ancestral halls
Which coil into each other, into you, into time

Love, forgive me at night, most of all at night:
Let me go back to the dance, the crowd

My body is a gun made of sorrow
aimed at you

Don't snag me into your trap
This is nothing compared to what I ran from

Sevgilim – beni o uzun masalara, o şık salonlara
Sevgilim – beni gündüzlerden kolla

Ölülerin sazlığından geçir, annenin yanağından
Çorabı kaçık kızlar zaten sabahın değil

II

Sevgilim – dinle beni geceleri, en çok geceleri
Zaten nasıl akar bu dilimdeki

Pıtraklı, çoklu, ayazlı
Bendeki ses öylesine değil

Sevgilim - beni şaraba yatır geceleri
Korkularından yont, yoksulluğundan damıt

Beni süsenlere söyle, yaseminlere beni
Beni semazenlere en çok, beni en çok geceleri

III

Sevgilim – beni dünya say, bir üzümden soy
Pergelin döndüğü bizden değil

Seni durmadan çarptığım o ağrıyı unut
Olduğu yerde kalsın uzak – onu unut

Bir elma olup bir sokak ağzında
Kahkaha olup patlamak kulaklarında

Love, save me from those mornings,
from those long tables, those elegant rooms

You could go swimming in the marshes of death
and still dive back freely into those mornings

with the approval of your mother's fine cheekbone,
me in my holey tights stumbling through breakfast.

II

Love, listen to me at night, most of all at night
So I can let these words fall from my tongue

Prickly threads of sound
Nothing like my voice

Love, night-times, lay me down on a bed of wine
Distilled from your poverty, poured from your fears

Tell the freesias and jasmines about me
And most of all tell the dervishes, especially at night

III

Love, see a world in me, a peeled grape
Ignore the spinning machinery outside

Forget the pain I keep pressing on you,
Let it rest, let it fade into the distance

Sevgilim – sen benim sesimden geçtin sularla
Yollarda düşürdüğün oysa cebinden değil

Öylece duran saksıda bekleyiş ne ki
Benim tozumun yanında

Düğmenin çözülüşüdür anlam
Sözdür, kime vursa öldürür

Sevgilim – eğil de bir bak bana
Yanına kıvrıldığın çoktur senden değil

Suyun da vakti yok nedense benimle akmaya
Kimse gelmeyecek işte - gecede duranı sabaha koymaya

Catch an apple, a burst of street talk, a catcall,
an explosion of laughter in your ear.

Love, you streamed through my voice like water
What you've dropped didn't fall from your pockets

Waiting, I've gathered more dust
Than an undisturbed vase

There is meaning in an undone button
It is words which kill their targets

Love, lean into me, look at me
You touch me but you left ages ago

Even water's too busy to flow with me
No one's coming to put a stop to the night, to let morning in.

ANGÉLICA FREITAS

O pavão no telhado

Ele voa. Está no teto
do alojamento, extraordinário
e ao mesmo tempo,
ave. Voa.
Não sabia. Não o conheço.
Isto é um retiro de meditação
em silêncio, dez dias de pavões
e nenhum comentário.
Os joelhos doem de ficar sentada
no chão tanto tempo.
No intervalo, a recompensa: um pavão
que abre a cauda, e todas,
sem emitir som, abrimos a boca.
Majestade, não vos conheço.
A primeira vez que o ouvi,
achei que fosse um gato
em apuros.
A instrução é ficar de olhos fechados.
Respiração, espirros, e o pavão
dando gritos. Depois, a cantoria
das mesquitas, e eu choro.
Não sei por quê, mas choro.
No último dia alguém encontra,
encantada, uma pena do bicho.
Vai levá-la para casa, guardá-la

ANGÉLICA FREITAS

The Peacock on the Roof

English version by Tara Bergin,
based on a literal translation from the Portuguese by Hilary Kaplan

It flies.
It's up there on the roof
of the hostel, extraordinary,
and at the same time,
a bird. Flying.
It's just I didn't know –
I don't know –
how.
I'm on a silent meditation retreat.
Ten days of peacocks and no one speaks.
My knees ache from sitting cross-legged on the floor.
But each day at break we get the reward:
a peacock, that opens out its tail
while we all silently open our mouths.
Power and Glory. I do not know you.
At first I think it is a cat in pain.
It has all its eyes open
but we are told to keep all our eyes closed.
There's the sound of breathing, sneezing,
the peacock screaming,
and then the call to prayer from the mosques
and I cry.
I don't know why, but I cry.
On the last day,
one woman finds a feather with an eye.

em algum livro sagrado.
Anos mais tarde, a lembrança
será a ave no teto, sua cauda aberta,
o silêncio de quarenta mulheres,
e não saber quase nada.
De nós mesmas,
da engenharia do vôo.

She's going to take it home and keep it in a sacred book.
Years from now it will remind her of the peacock
on the roof, its tail spread bright;
and of the forty silent women
who didn't know that much about themselves,
or the mechanics of flight.

حافظ موسوی

نام آن پرنده‌ی غمگین

بانوی پارسی، از غسل کودکش در آفتاب سحرگاهی برمی‌گردد
و از کنار خاکستر کلبه‌ی بوسیس و فیلمون، تلخ می‌گذرد.
(از استخوان‌های سوخته‌ی آن دو و میهمان‌شان هنوز دود برمی‌خیزد.)
آقای فاووست با چشم‌های خیس و دلی لرزان،
از اوج برج، بر قلمرو بی‌انتهای خویش، فاتحانه می‌نگرد.
«سرود شادی» با روشن‌ترین واژه‌ها، در آسمان اروپا طنین می‌اندازد.
گوته، خیره در چشم‌های دخترک شعر آسمانی هاینه
آخرین جمله‌اش را می‌نویسد و قلم را بر زمین می‌گذارد:
«زنانگی جاودانه، به فراز بر می‌کشاندمان. درستش این است.»

آنک «سرود شادی» در افق دوردست رو به خاموشی‌ست.
بانوی سالخورده، در جامه‌ای سیاه به صحنه می‌آید
و ارواح مردگان را به صحنه فرا می‌خواند.
تالار، زیر بارش نت‌های خاکستری، تاریک می‌شود.
طنین آشنای «فوگ مرگ» شانه‌ی ارواح را به لرزه می‌اندازد.
گروه همسرایان می‌خوانند:
«آه شیلر! شیلر عزیز!»
این روح شاعری‌ست که موهای مادرش هرگز به سپیدی نرسید.
(و او همان کسی‌ست که شیر سیاه سپیده‌دمان را نوشید و در تابوت آب سفر کرد.)
این روح مردگانی‌ست که مرگ از استخوان‌های پوک‌شان نی‌لبک می‌ساخت.

HAFEZ MOUSAVI

The Name of that Sad Dove

English version by Daisy Fried,
based on a literal translation from the Persian by Alireza Abiz

The Parsi couple returning from bathing their baby under the
　　morning sun
sadly passes the ashes of Baucis' and Philemon's hut,
smoke still rising from their burnt bones, and from their guest's bones.
Weepy, heavy in his heart, Herr Faust surveys
his endless dominion from the top of his tower
as *Ode to Joy* rings out in European skies. *God sparks!*
Heine's muse had the most heavenly eyes – Goethe gazes there,
writes his last sentence, puts his pencil down:
Eternal Womanhood leads us higher.

Ode to Joy fades in the distance.
An old lady takes the stage dressed in black
and summons ghosts of the dead.
The hall darkens, the music becomes grey rain.
Todesfuge shakes the ghosts.
Oh Schiller! Dear Schiller! the chorus sings.
This is the ghost of Antschel-Celan whose mother's hair never
　　turned white
she's the one who drank the black milk of morning and travelled to a
　　grave in the clouds.
These are the ghosts of those from whose hollow bones death began to
　　whittle his flutes.

آن دیگری زنی‌ست، فاحشه‌ای که زیر رگباری از تگرگ، کودکی مرده می‌زاید.
اینان «بافندگان شلزی»اند که برای تمدن ما کفن می‌بافند.
آن دیگران، دیوانگانی‌اند بر کرانه‌ی دریای دور شب‌زده
چشم انتظار پاسخی که نیست؛ هرگز نبوده است.

و این یکان، پلنگان‌اند، همان پلنگان در قفس ریلکه
و گاه، فیلی سفید، یکی فیل، چرخان، چرخان، چرخان
و آنان، دوشیزگانی که بر کرانه‌ی دریا به تماشای شفق ایستاده‌اند
و «آه کشیدن» را از یاد برده‌اند
و هیچ یک نمی‌دانند، که نام آن پرنده‌ی غمگین
کز قلب‌ها گریخته، «ایمان» است.

This other is the one they call whore, whose child is born dead in icy
    convulsions.
These are the Silesian Weavers, weaving civilisation our funeral
    shrouds.
Those other fools wait by the sea, by the dumb dead night-coloured sea,
for an answer that never has, will never, come.

And this is the panther, Rilke's caged panther.
And now and then, a white elephant moves, turns, circles.
And at the seaside, the young people are watching the sunset
who have forgotten how to sigh,
and no one knows
the name of the sad dove that's flown their hearts is *faith*.

NOTE: 'The Name of that Sad Dove' references or quotes directly from a number of
German and Persian poems, the detailed sources for which can be found on page 159.

CLARA JANÉS

Canto del Escanciador

Todavía llegan las rosas de Shiraz a mi poema
y el canto de aquel loco de Dios junto a la alberca mientras el día
    declinaba,
y llega a mis manos la esmaltada copa del poeta.
Como en la de Djamshid, el cosmos todo se desliza en su víno
y destellan las constelaciones, y su danza dibuja la armonía
entre el hombre y la piedra, el animal y la planta,
y aquellas hojas, que en el *orto* de Padua indican metamórfosis.

Que todo cambia y los tiempos escapan lo enuncian las campanillas
    de las caravanas,
pero la mente del que contempla y piensa galopa en traslación
pues 'abanico es la palabra!,' y cuenta del rosario del amor y de la
    ciencia.

¡Sírveme, escanciador, sirve otra copa!, para que vea con detalle
todos los reflejos y, junto al amado y los textos sabios,
lea con mansedumbre activa el universo, ya que mirándolos los creo.

Como en el átomo, en torno a la carga positiva, bailan los electrones,
y en el cosmos expande la función de ondas una trama sin fin,
los bucles de un secreto amado revelan los ocultos lazos
entre lo existente, borrando abismos de sujeto y objeto.

CLARA JANÉS

The Song of the One Who Pours the Wine

English version by Lavinia Greenlaw,
based on a literal translation from the Spanish by Catherine Mansfield

The roses of Shiraz still climb through this page
as does the song of the holy fool who stands at dusk by the well.
The decorated cup of the poet appears in my hands.
Like the cup of Jamshid, it contains worlds
within the depths of its wine.
The ripple of submerged constellations reveals a pattern
shared by flora and fauna, what is human and what is stone.
You see it in the palm leaves in the botanical garden at Padua,
a famous illustration of metamorphosis.

There is a formula chimed in the caravan's tiny bells:
all must change, time must pass. Even so
the mind of one who contemplates must fix it all in place
(A word's a fan!) and strings together prayer beads of science, of love.

Pour me another cup! I want to see in detail
All that swims in reflection. I will read the cosmos
as a sacred text – accepting that what I see, I have to believe.

Like electrons held in the dance around an atom's positive charge
or the endless extension and connection of the wave,
the deep secret of this circuitry reveals the link
between all that exists, collapsing space between subject and object.

Todo esto resumen exhalando las rosas de Shiraz,
cuyo amor es perfume y tablilla del primer alfabeto
que pregona todavía en Persépolis la dignidad del hombre.

Sí, mientras declina el día y canta aquel loco de Dios, junto a la alberca,
recibo la llama del fuego del saber de la mano del poeta
y exclamo con él una vez más: '¡Sea mi única dicha pulsarte, naturaleza!'

All this is held in the perfume exhaled by the roses of Shiraz,
a perfume that is love, that is the writing of the first alphabet
which in Persepolis declares our human grace.

Yes, as dusk falls and the holy fool sings by the well,
the poet places a flicker from the blaze of all that is known in my hands
and together we repeat his invocation: Nature, my one joy is to connect!

فاضل العزاوي

الجنة فوق الأرض

في العتمة ليلا وأنا أخرج سكران من الحانة
أترنح في خطواتي، فيما ثمة أشباح تتعقبني
وكلاب هائجة تنبح خلفي
رحت أغني كالمجنون بأعلى صوتي
كي أنسى وحشة دربي.

أوقفني درويش في زي ملاك في تكية
بعصا يحملها هددني، وبخني أني بددت حياتي بين الحانات سدى
ثم دعاني ورعا:
- افلا تعرف يا آدم؟ ممنوع أن تسكر في هذي الدنيا
فاذهب واشرب خمرك مجانا في الجنة
صحبة أجمل حوريات العالم!
- آه، ولكن قل لي أين تكون الجنة يا سيد أيامي؟
بعصاه أشار الى نجم دري يتلألأ في الأبدية:
- في أعلى عليين!
ثم مضى مختالا كالصقر يرفرف نحو الله وطار.

فلبثت مكاني لا أعرف ماذا أفعل
حتى باغتني الشاعر حافظ يضحك مسرورا
وهو يعود من الحانة مثلي:
- لا تحزن يا صاحب عمري إن كانت جنتهم عالية الأسوار
وأنت بلا أجنحة لتطير اليها
إذ نحن هنا أيضا نقدر أن نبني فوق الأرض الجنة
فلنا غابات تمتد بعيدا ومراع خضراء
أنهار جارية وجبال نصعدها حين يجيء الطوفان

FADHIL AL-AZZAWI

Paradise on Earth

English version by Jorie Graham,
based on a literal translation from the Arabic by the author

As I leave the tavern, I see it, the dark of the night.
Each step I take shakes me. An evil spirit follows me.
Furious dogs bark. They come from behind. They hunt me.
I must forget the solitude of this road.
I must sing like a madman. I must sing louder.

Disguised as an angel now, a dervish slips out of the mosque.
He threatens me. His stick waves in the air.
You are losing your life he screams. *You have lost your life.*
Adam, Adam, don't you know it's forbidden to drink
in this world. Go drink the wine of Paradise in Paradise.
Go drink that wine, it's bountiful, it's free of charge.
Go find the beautiful-eyed houris, the bountiful houris, free of charge.

Oh master of my days, show me this place, where is this place?

It's then he points his stick up to the star. *There* he says. *Eternity.*
I watch it twinkle, blaze. *Up there*, he says, fluttering like a falcon,
rising, resplendent and disappearing.

I do not move. What should I do? I do not move.
Hafiz the poet surprises me, laughing,
arriving suddenly as always upon me from our tavern.
My friend, he laughs, why worry? Look up, their walls are so high,
and you, you have no wings to fly there – no –

وبحار تزخر أسماكا ومحيطات تلهو فيها الحيتان
فتيات من أجمل ما خلق الله تعالى
والحية نجلبها أيضا في قفص كي تتسلق أغصان الشجرة
ماذا نطلب أكثر من ذلك؟

let us turn this earth into the paradise,
look at these woods stretching away, these meadows, running rivers,
look at our mountains rising up for when the flood comes,
and these seas, these oceans full of swirling fish, dancing whales,
these most beautiful of creatures, these houris created by God,
and let us not forget to release the snake from its cage
to entwine the branches of our glorious tree –
what more will we need
than that?

JAN WAGNER

ephesusghasele

Und er lief, da war der Tore
Wart' und Turm und alles anders.
Goethe, *West-östlicher Divan*

ein früher tod war ja erwartbar
bei einem kaiser, der so hart war
in glaubensfragen (maler stellen
ihn kalten blicks und stark behaart dar).
so waren sieben junge männer
im hals- und handumdrehen startklar
und auf der flucht, versteckten sich,
bevor die nacht zum tag geklart war,
in einer höhle – samt dem hund,
der in die sieben ganz vernarrt war.
dort schliefen sie. der kaiser ließ,
als fels um fels herangekarrt war,
das loch vermauern, doch sie schliefen,
woche um woche, quint- um quartjahr,
jahrhunderte, jahrhunderte,
so tief, daß schlaf mit tod gepaart war
oder so schien, und eine hand,
die ungeheuerlich, doch zart war,
drehte sie um im schlaf bei dem,
was höhlen- oder himmelfahrt war.

JAN WAGNER

Ephesus Ghazal

English version by Robin Robertson,
based on a literal translation from the German by Iain Galbraith

Then he ran. Now the gateway,
towers, turrets, all looked different.
Goethe, 'The Seven Sleepers', *West-Eastern Divan*

An early death was considered likely
with an emperor so hard, so severe
in matters of belief, that painters showed him
shaggy-faced, with eyes like sleet.
And so the seven of them, seven young men,
prepared for a quick escape, to flee –
and when they did, they hid themselves
before morning, before the night had cleared,
in a cave – together with the dog
who loved them all, and curled up at their feet.
And there they slept. Meanwhile, the emperor
ordered cartloads of rocks to the breach
and the cave blocked up, but still they slept,
week after week, years upon years,
for centuries, *centuries,*
so deeply, that death was twined with sleep
or seemed that way – and an angel's hand,
dreadful, delicate, turned them gently
on his way to heaven or down to hell,
rolling each one over in their sleep.

hungrig erwachten sie. kein fels mehr,
doch glaubten sie, was offenbart war,
sei nur der tag, schickten zur stadt
den jüngsten, der geschickt und smart war,
statt strafgericht den bäcker fand,
der überrascht und wie erstarrt war,
die freunde alarmierte – denn
der münze, lange aufgespart, war
ein toter kaiser eingraviert.
wer zweifelte? um ihn geschart war
die ganze stadt, bestaunte ihn,
der fern der zeit und doch apart war,
dessen geschlecht mit onkeln, enkeln
und ururenkeln längst verscharrt war,
nichts als ein staub, derweil er selbst
noch immer jung und ohne bart war,
sein eigner, letzter erbe, der
äonen alt, doch nicht bejahrt war.
so ließ man töpfe köcheln, zog,
bevor die hirse ganz gegart war,
von ephesus zur höhle, fand
ein volk von sieben, dem erspart war
zu sterben, fand mit ihm und ihm
und ihm und ihm und ihm und ihm,
was vorerst für die ewigkeit bewahrt war.

They woke hungry, the rocks all crumbled away,
thinking the new morning they could see
was just one night old, and sent to town
the youngest – skilful and keen –
who found a baker's where the court used to be.
The baker was startled, paralysed with fear,
calling his friends: for on the proferred coin –
long-hoarded – was the face, engraved and clear,
of an emperor dead for hundreds of years.
Who could doubt it? Around him, crowds seethed;
the whole town, marvelling at him,
this boy from the past, yet standing here,
whose people – uncles, grandchildren,
great-grandchildren – all long buried,
were nothing but dust, while he himself
was still young, still trying for a beard,
his own final heir: aeons old,
but *not* old, not even elderly.
So they set pots simmering, and left Ephesus
before the millet was ready,
heading for the cave, and found there
a clan of seven: spared – freed
from dying – found with him and him
and him and him and him and him
held for eternity; for the time being.

ESSAYS

Bringing Persia to Germany:
Joseph von Hammer and Hafiz

SIBYLLE WENTKER

My little book makes plain in all its parts
how indebted I am to this estimable man.

Johann Wolfgang von Goethe,
West-Eastern Divan, 'Von Hammer'

It is a well-known and oft-repeated fact that the initial spark for Goethe's *West-Eastern Divan* came from his reading of Hammer's translation of Shams ad-Din Hafiz's Persian Divan into the German language. As Goethe writes, he instantly developed the wish to connect with Hafiz through literary production of his own. Goethe had used publications by Hammer before. He mentions the journal *Fundgruben des Orients* (Treasure-trove of the Orient), which Hammer edited in the years 1809–18 and also his Persian literary history, the *Geschichte der schönen Redekünste Persiens* (History of the Beautiful Arts of Persian Rhetoric) which was published in 1818. Both works Goethe valued highly, as he writes in his 'Notes And Essays for a Better Understanding of the *West-Eastern Divan*'.[1]

How greatly Goethe was inspired by the motto of the *Fundgruben*, 'Sag: Gottes ist der Orient, Gottes ist der Okzident, er leitet, wen er will, den wahren Pfad', becomes visible in one of the most famous poems in the *West-östlicher Divan*:

To God belongs the Orient! To God belongs the Occident!
Northern and southern lands rest in the peace of His hands.[2]

Joseph von Hammer's place in German scholarship in regard to his contribution to Goethe's *West-Eastern Divan* is substantial. Interestingly enough this is not generally recognised in the scholarly history of the period. The accolade accorded to Hammer's work by the Titan of German literature Johann Wolfgang von Goethe did not, paradoxically enough, lead to a thorough treatment of Joseph von Hammer and his work. Exceptions to this rule are the works by Ingeborg Solbrig, Nima Mina and, to some extent, Hamid Tafazoli.[3] In general Hammer's role is limited to giving Goethe the idea for the *West-Eastern Divan*. The downplaying of Hammer goes hand in hand with the downplaying of the quality of his translations. The harsh verdicts of his contemporaries, often imposed out of personal animosity, went on being repeated by scholars of German studies, although themselves ignorant of Oriental languages, among them Hendrik Birus, who classified Hammer's translation as: 'an sich wenig inspiriert' (in itself offering little inspiration).[4] But also scholars of Persian and Arabic continued to misclassify Hammer's translation of Hafiz as a minor and outdated contribution to its field. Hartmut Bobzin, for example, wrote in a review about the 2003 reprint of the 1812–13 edition: 'Daß im übrigen Hammers Übersetzung in fast jeder Hinsicht überholt ist und ihren (freilich begrenzten) Wert lediglich als "Quelle" für Goethes *Divan*-Inspiration besitzt, sei am Rande vermerkt' (It should be noted by the way that Hammer's translation is outdated in almost every sense and that its (limited) value lies in acting as 'source' for Goethe's *Divan*-inspiration).[5] This article opposes such downplaying and attempts to acknowledge the quality of Hammer's translation of Hafiz given the time in which it was done and what was then possible.

Joseph von Hammer (1774–1856), Hammer-Purgstall after 1835, was without exaggeration the most eminent scholar of Oriental Studies Austria can boast. This is due to his tremendous productivity on the one hand and the vast variety of his interests and activities on the other. It is hard to imagine any scholarly enterprise concerning Oriental matters in the first half of the nineteenth century without Hammer-Purgstall being involved. Born in Graz, Styria, Hammer moved at a young age to Vienna and enrolled in the Oriental Academy, a school founded by Maria Theresa in 1754 with the goal of educating interpreters and diplomats in Oriental languages for the foreign service. For his entire professional life Hammer remained a civil servant of the Staatskanzlei (the foreign ministry), although he was able to devote much of his time to scholarly matters. This was not unusual, there are several examples of Austrian diplomats trained at the Oriental Academy who published on various scholarly matters. What makes Hammer outstanding is the intensity of his studies, which easily outpaced his peers'. Due to the lack of proper language-instruction material and also due to the mode of the time, the language was taught via poetry. During his time at the Oriental Academy Hammer read a vast amount of poetry; in his memoirs he writes that he read a billion lines. In addition to the work of other Persian, Turkish and Arabic poets Hammer encountered the work of the most famous Persian poet, Hafiz. From 1798 on he spent regular evenings reading Hafiz together with his school friend Karl von Harrach. In 1799 Hammer was transferred to Constantinople, and there he heard for the first time a Persian recite verses of Hafiz 'Es war der erste Perser, den ich seine Muttersprache sprechen und Hafiz lesen hörte. Im Besitz eines Diwan's desselben mit dem Kommentar Sudi's fasste ich den Entschluss der Übersetzung ins Deutsche.' (He was the first Persian I heard speaking his mother tongue and reading Hafiz. In possession of the *Divan* itself and with Sudi's commentary I made the decision to translate it into German').[6] The similarity to Goethe is striking, in that the reading or listening to Hafiz becomes the starting point for translation or poetic production. It is hard to say if this passage in his memoirs, which by the way do not contain many references to Goethe, is shaped according to the latter's words in his 'Notes and Essays' quoted above. In the introduction to his translation Hammer states plainly that he began the translation in 1799 and finished it in 1806.[7]

Hammer's translation was, in fact, the first translation of the complete text into German. The celebrated William Jones had incorporated translations of single lines of Hafiz in his *A Grammar of the Persian Language* and also in his *Dissertation sur la littérature orientale* (Dissertation on Oriental Literature),[8] where he compared the verses of Hafiz with those of Horace.[9] Also in 1771 the Austrian diplomat of Hungarian origin, Karl Emmerich Revicky, translated poems of Hafiz into Latin and commented on the poems verse by verse. Hammer writes in his introduction that he translated aproximately seven hundred poems by Hafiz from the divan.

*

The importance of Hafiz, Shams ad-Din Muhammad Shirazi (*c.* 1315–90),[10] for Persian literary history and identity cannot be overestimated. Even today in every literary Persian house, Hafiz is regarded as the Titan of Persian literature, as Goethe would be that of German literature. However, whereas even today almost every Persian-speaking person can recite some verse by Hafiz, it is unlikely that the average German could do the same by Goethe. This difference is important because it shows the importance accorded to literature in general in Iranian culture.

Hafiz is recognised for his unmatched mastery of the nuances of Persian language in combination with a remarkable sense for rhythm and musicality, which is important for memorising the verses easily. Hammer translated Hafiz' poetry into verse, trying to reshape the Persian text into German. Hafiz's favorite form of poem is the *ghazal*, which is the form for love poetry. Hafiz uses the *ghazal* for love poetry as well, he shapes verses of unrequited love and affection for the young and beautiful *Saqi*, the cupbearer in wine houses. Thematically Hafiz opens the possibility of topics for his *ghazals* on drinking poems. '. . . no other poet made bacchanalia so frequent and integral a part of his poetry.'[11] In addition to wine and love Hafiz includes poems in which he exposes as hypocritical, often in a very witty and funny way, the superficially pious man who preaches water and drinks wine. His attacks always target the authorities. The poems challenge the self-declared authority of the officials of the time and unmask their obliquity. As Ehsan Yarshater writes: 'The wittiest lines of Hafiz are those in which he attacks the false figures of authority in the institutional religion.' And further: 'One of the main reasons for the popularity of Hafiz is precisely his trenchant gibes against the pretenders of piety in the religious establishment.' Yarshater belongs to the fraction of scholars who oppose the popular opinion that Hafiz's poetry contains secret mystical content (*lisan al-ghayb*, lit. the tongue of the unseen). 'Attempts at finding a mystical interpretation for Hafiz's praise of wine and drunkenness are not supported by his Divan.'[12]

Reducing Hafiz to the free-thinking rebel against the religious and stately authorities alone, has been opposed by many, prominently by Annemarie Schimmel, who stressed the multifaceted and manifold possibilities of interpretation of Hafiz's poetry. She was very much convinced that Hafiz's poetry was strongly embedded in the mystical literary tradition of Shiraz and had a strong mystical element and gave several examples of the diverse possibilities for interpreting his poems.[13]

For the European reader during the romantic development of the enlightenment idea of freedom of thought, this aspect of Hafiz's poetry was especially favourable. John D. Yohannan goes so far as to say: 'Hafiz in the Age of Reason could only be perceived as a sort of pseudo-classical lyrist – the "Persian Anacreon".'[14] Goethe was strongly attracted by the anti-authoritarian attitude suggested by Hammer's translation, but this did not prevent him from interpreting Hafiz more broadly than Hammer, as we can see in the poetry of the *West-Eastern Divan*:

> But you are mystically pure because they do not understand you – you who without being pious, are blessed! They will never concede you that.[15]

The key phrase for me is to be blessed without being pious. The independent, free, uninfluenced by orthodox theology Hafiz seemed for Goethe to be the ideal twin. This did not hinder Goethe from seeing the mystical dimension in the poetry, as Annemarie Schimmel has stated, where she quotes Goethe's famous poem 'Selige Sehnsucht' (Holy Longing) in the first book of the *Divan* as an example of the mystic's strive to dissolve like the butterfly into eternity.[16]

The form of Hafiz's *ghazal*s is apparently simple, but they employ an artful language which the connoisseur is able to enjoy up to the level of his knowledge, whereas the beginner is not. This makes the pleasure of Persian poetry an exclusive and educated one. Only if the reader is able to decipher the manifold metaphors and images of speech, can he understand the *ghazals* in all their facets. As Ingeborg Solbrig has written, 'Ohne Einführung ist dem westlichen Leser die Bedeutung der Symbolik oder Allegorie, die streng festliegt, nicht zugänglich' (The meaning of the imagery or allegory, which is strictly defined, is inaccessible to the Western reader without introduction).[17] Joseph von Hammer, we should remember, had acquired through his intense reading of Persian poetry a more than solid grasp of the way metaphorical language works. He – and this gave his critics ammunition – denied the mystical component of Hafiz's *ghazals*. In 1818 he wrote:

Desto weniger verdiente er aber seinen Vor- und später hinzuge-
kommenen Eigenschaftsnamen, denn dem Glauben hat er als
Sonne schlecht vorgeleuchtet, und seine Zunge dollmetschte bloß
die Lehren des Sinnesgenusses, und nicht die Mysterien der
göttlichen Liebe. [. . .] so ist doch die Gesamtheit seiner Gedichte
nichts, als ein lauter Aufruf zu Liebe und Wein, und der höchste
Ausbruch erotischer und bachantischer Begeisterung (The less he
deserved his name and his later appellative name [*Hammer refers
to Shams ad-Din 'Sun of religion' and* lisan al-ghayb *(tongue of the
unseen)*] since his tongue interpreted only the doctrine of pleasure
and not the mysteries of divine love. [. . .][18] His poetry in its
entirety is nothing more than a loud call for love and wine, and
it is the highest outburst of erotic and bacchantic enthusiasm).

Hammer's view of Persian literature was very much influenced by the
way the Ottoman Empire valued literature. Hafiz and Persian literature
in general was very popular in the Ottoman Empire. Ottoman Turkish
was greatly enriched by Persian idioms and figures of speech. Persian and
the Persian style of letter writing was copied in the Ottoman Empire,
where the use of the elaborate Persian style was regarded as beautiful.
Ottoman commentaries helped the average or even the advanced reader
in understanding the difficulties of the Persian texts. Also Hammer used
a commentary on Hafiz. Of three standard commentaries, he chose that
of Ahmad Sudi (*d.* 1591). Sudi is said to be one of the most prominent
Ottoman Persianists.[19] Originally from Eastern Bosnia, he was educated
in Diyarbakir and later served as a teacher at the Ibrahim Pasha Madrasa
in Istanbul, where he wrote several commentaries on Persian poets. His
commentaries, including that on Hafiz, are philologically focused. He
does not follow the popular trend to attribute a 'hidden' mystical mean-
ing to his wordly verses about song and love. As Brockhaus writes in his
edition of the commentary of Sudi: ‚Sudi erklärt den Hafiz als Philolog
und mit warmem Gefühle für die Schönheiten der Dichtung, nicht als
Theolog' (Sudi elucidates Hafiz as a philologist, with a warm sense of
the beauty of the poetry, not as a theologian).[20] This attitude had a strong
influence on Hammer's view of Hafiz. So he writes in his introduction:
'Der Uebersetzer ist in die Fußstapfen Sudi's getreten' (The translator

walks in Sudi's footsteps).[21] This commitment to a wordly interpretation has earned Hammer the accusation of one-dimensionality, which reduces the complexity of Hafiz's poetry to drinking and sensual pleasures.

Nima Mina is the first to have actually tried to analyse the quality and the general achievements of Hammer's translation, something most Germanists were simply not able to do. He observed that Hammer translated verse by verse, and that the translation follows rhythmical patterns, but is not rhymed at the end. For Mina the mastery of a rhetorical vocabulary, which can be interpreted in either a mystical or a wordly way, especially when it comes to wine and love, is part of the poet's general repertoire of the time. The use of themes and motives coming out of the Sufic tradition does not necessarily mean that Hafiz himself was part of mystic environments.[22] Hammer, opposing any Sufic content in Hafiz's poetry, chose the interpretation of mundane love, even when clear signs of mystical-religious content are visible.[23] He stresses that Hammer, although he understood very well the countless ambiguities in the text, normally chose the superficial interpretation, whereas he had no problem acknowledging the male sex of Hafiz's beloved, which so many others have turned into a woman.[24] On the whole, Mina judges the quality of Hammer's translations to be very high. He goes so far as to say that the existing philological mistakes in the translation are due to the mistakes of the editor Sudi.[25] Annemarie Schimmel, although opposing Hammer's 'mundane' translation, says similarly that the mistakes in the text can be put down to printing errors.

In Hammer's time the book was praised, but it, or rather Hammer, also met with strong disapproval. In today's light these criticisms may seem a bit silly, but in their time the confrontation was fought with remarkable vigour, and, as observed at the beginning of this essay, this has had consequences for the reputation of Hammer's work until today.

We do not know, what Hammer thought about the *West-Eastern Divan*, but we do know that Karl August Böttiger, an influential personality in Weimar who from 1804 lived in Dresden, following a serious disagreement with Goethe, was in regular correspondence with Hammer, telling him eagerly the gossip of the town. On 4 November 1818 he wrote to Hammer: 'Sahen Sie denn schon Goethes Diwan? Man spricht mir mit

Entzücken davon. Offenbar hat er Ihren Hafiz nun auf seine Weise ausgeborgt und in Ihr Nest seine Eier gelegt. Noch habe ichs nicht zu Gesicht bekommen. Ich wünschte sehr, Ihre Ansicht darüber zu erfahren.' (Did you see Goethe's *Divan* already? Everybody speaks of it with delight. Obviously he borrowed your Hafiz in his way and put his egg in your nest. I have not seen it yet, I would love to hear your opinion about it.)[26]

Hammer's answer, if he gave one, is unknown. In the autobiography Hammer wrote thirty years later, he mentions very dryly among his readings in the summer 1819: '[...] von Dichterwerken den Childe Harold und Goethe's westöstlichen Diwan durchgenommen und durchgenossen' ([. . .] studied and enjoyed among works of poetry *Childe Harold* and Goethe's *West-Eastern Divan*).[27]

It seems to me of some relevance that Goethe's *West-Eastern Divan* is in its setting and composition a Persian book. The poetic part is structured by a series of *nameh*, the Persian word for book. The Persian character of the *West-Eastern Divan* is probably disguised a little bit by the fact that Goethe's 'Notes and Essays' cover a *tour d'horizon* through Goethe's general readings on this topic, which includes a broader cosmos of Oriental Studies than only Persian literature. Goethe's wish to mediate Persian literature into the German in the *West-Eastern Divan* has been estimated in recent times as a desire to overcome differences of an intercultural kind. Joseph von Hammer, who brought a significant part of Persian culture and identity, Hafiz's poems, to Romantic Germany, should not be forgotten.

Goethe and 'the East' of Today

RAJMOHAN GANDHI

'East' and 'West' are popular and often useful categories, but how the terms are understood can vary from decade to decade, or place to place. There was a time when people in Goa on India's west coast, or in Mozambique on Africa's east coast, imagined 'Portugal' when 'the West' was mentioned, while persons elsewhere thought of Spain, Belgium, Holland, France or England.

After the Second World War in the last century, 'the West' to many meant the United States, and the 'East versus West' phrase frequently signified the Soviet-American conflict. Yet in the first decade of the same century, when Japan and Russia clashed, Russia was 'the West' not only to most Japanese, but also to other Asians. When Japan won, Asians including Indians felt glad that after two centuries of European trading companies ruling over much of the Orient, an Asian country had finally triumphed over 'the West'.

Goethe wrote his *West-Eastern Divan* in the period between 1814 and 1819, exactly one hundred years before the First World War years. His *Divan*'s 'East' was the Muslim East, more a religio-cultural space than a geographical bloc of nations. However, Islamic Turkey, Islamic Egypt and Islamic Iran must also have seemed physically remote to most Europeans. Interestingly, Goethe in his *Divan* seemed to assume a commonness, bestowed by Islam, among Arabs, Persians and Turks.

If they are even faintly aware of recent headlines – about the Rohingya, for instance, or of attacks on religious minorities in India, Pakistan, Bangladesh or Sri Lanka – few today would see 'the East' and 'the Muslim world' as synonyms. And fewer would lump Arabs, Persians and Turks together. Not when Arab lands, Israel and the USA seem aligned on one side, and Iran and Palestinians on the other, while Turkey hobbles somewhere in between.

A phenomenon like Goethe is not likely to re-emerge in our times. If he does, a twenty-first-century Goethe might need to compose more than a dozen *divans* merely to foster dialogue inside the Muslim world, and dozens more to get 'West' and 'East' to know each other!

Today 'the West' too, howsoever understood, is a splintered category, while the Muslim 'East' is brutally divided. Other Eastern spaces, whether Buddhist, Hindu, Confucian, Sikh or whatever, are also at odds with one another. As former president Barack Obama recently said to a close aide, 'Maybe people just want to fall back into their tribe.'[1]

Fully aware of the difference between 'Muslim' and 'Eastern', Goethe ignored labels in order to expose realities common to all. One can only marvel at his cheek, early in the nineteenth century, in telling fellow-Europeans that in their predicaments or longings they were like Muslims. Wrote Goethe in his *Divan*:

> How foolish that everyone praises his own opinion in what pertains to him. If *Islam* means submission to God, we all are living and dying in Islam.[2]

Expressing an insight like this, I suspect, was probably as unusual in the Europe of the 1810s as it would be today. For one thing, the defeat and death in 1799 of England's stubborn foe, Tipu Sultan of Mysore, was for Europe a recent and also a greatly celebrated event. Mysore's ruler had been portrayed as a cruel and resourceful Muslim fanatic as dangerous to England as Napoleon whom the British would defeat in 1815 at Waterloo.

It was fully expected, moreover, that Napoleon and Tipu would join hands and fight the British together. In the end, the Duke of Wellington who proved victorious in Waterloo (in 'the West') was the very Arthur Wellesley who sixteen years earlier had played a crucial role in Tipu's fall in Mysore (in 'the East').

In such a climate of phobia, Goethe expressed a courageous thought. He said that in wanting human beings to obey God and respect one another, the prophet of Islam was only urging what Jesus and Moses had prescribed.

The Goethe saying this was now in his sixties. His supremely successful novels and poems, as also his scientific and administrative accomplishments, had brought him an exceptional stature. Even so his *Divan* sold poorly. His fellow-Europeans were not enthusiastic about recognising Islam's virtues.

It would appear that in addition to being prodigiously gifted, Goethe was honest. He loved Rumi's verses as also the later output of Hafiz, the fourteenth-century Persian poet, which he had read in a German translation. He appeared to respond positively to a page in the Qur'an, brought from Spain by a soldier in the Napoleonic wars, which asked the reader-listener to seek refuge in God. Conducted by Bashkir soldiers arriving from Russia, an Islamic prayer service in a Weimar auditorium seemed to impress Goethe.[3] Liking what he encountered in Islam, the honest Goethe said so in his book's verses, which sailed with grace and could be read with ease.

A little more than a century later, Muhammad Iqbal (1876–1938), one of South Asia's greatest poets and the man who would give Pakistan its ideological foundation, ran into the *Divan*. Iqbal at this point was someone shaken by the Muslim world's pathetic situation. In *Shikwah* ('Complaint'), he had levelled a charge at the Almighty.

> There are nations beside us; there are sinners among
>   them too,
> Humble folk and those intoxicated with pride, slothful,
>   careless and clever,
> Hundreds who detest Thy Name,
> But Thy Grace descends on their dwelling;
> And nothing but the lightning strikes us![4]

When Iqbal wrote these lines, India's Muslims were facing, many of them thought, a double humiliation: rule by the West and likely rule in the future by India's majority Hindus, relations with whom had long been fraught.

Iqbal was bowled over by Goethe's cheerful appreciation in his *Divan* of Islam's message of submission to God. The *Divan* evoked from him the remarkable *Payam-i-Mashriq* ('The Message of the East'), which was published in 1923. Here are some of the *Payam*'s lines (translated by M. Hadi Hussain):

Do not come to my garden if you have
An uninquiring mind, which does not crave
To know the souls of flowers. My spring is not
Mere smell and colour, no mere surface wave.

A wonderful show, God, is Your world. All
Things seem to have drunk from the same wine-bowl.
Eye intimate with eye; but heart from heart
And soul from soul divided by a wall.

Life keeps expressing itself in new ways:
Content with one fixed form it never stays.
You have no spark in you if your today
Is just a copy of your yesterdays.

You ask how close the link between my soul
And body: that link is beyond compute.
Mere swirling, choked-up breath while in it, I
Am music when I issue from the flute.[5]

A century has passed since Iqbal wrote the Persian originals of these verses, which was a century after Goethe had written his *Divan*. The *Divan* and the *Payam* seem to converse with each other while descending the steps of time.

India's greatest modern poet, and a playwright, artist and composer as well, Rabindranath Tagore (1861–1941), who received the Nobel Prize for Literature in 1913, made visits in the 1920s to Germany, where he was most warmly received. Books of his poems translated into German were widely sold. I have however not managed to locate a reaction by Tagore to the *Divan*, which does not mean that he never voiced it.

Nor am I aware of a response by Mohandas Gandhi to the *Divan*, though the *Divan*'s gesture of boldly removing the locks to inter-faith dialogue was certainly reproduced more than once by Gandhi. We know in addition that Gandhi studied Goethe's *Faust* during his first incarceration by the British in India, which occurred from March 1922 to February 1924. In a notebook he procured in Pune's Yeravada prison, Gandhi copied these words of Gretchen (Margaret) from *Faust:*

> My poor sick brain is crazed with pain
> And my poor sick heart is torn in twain.[6]

*

The conversation noted above between Goethe and Iqbal had in fact started centuries earlier with Hafiz, Shiraz's deathless poet who lived in the fourteenth century. After the Mongols destroyed much of Iran in the thirteenth century, a brief stable phase was followed by a chain of petty dynasties in the next century, until Timur the fierce (Tamerlane), also possessing Mongol blood, conquered Persia's Shiraz and Esfahan and set much of India too on fire.

Creativity did not insist on a peaceful world. It was in the heated Timurid era that Hafiz composed the poetry that would engage future generations in and beyond Iran. In the 1810s, it would inspire Goethe. We are told that soon after Goethe read Hafiz, 'a storm of verses would break forth from him – two, three and more poems a day, on trips, at an inn, amid conversations and other activities'.[7]

We learn, too, that Goethe declined requests to write poems summoning nationalist passions, explaining his position in these words:

> How could I write songs of hatred when I felt no hate? . . . I never hated the French, although I thanked God when we were rid of them. How could I, to whom the only significant things are civilisation and barbarism, hate a nation which is among the most cultivated in the world, and to which I owe a great part of my own culture?[8]

Acknowledging the existence of hate at some levels, Goethe added:

> But there exists a level at which it wholly disappears, and where one stands, so to speak, above the nations, and feels the weal or woe of a neighbouring people as though it were one's own.[9]

Isn't this the key for our world today, a wish to feel a neighbour's pain as our own? On his part, Iqbal seemed to say something similar when he asked us to realise

> that life cannot effect a revolution in its environment before it has had, in the first instance, a revolution in the inner depths of its being, nor can a new world assume external form until its existence takes shape in the hearts of men.

In support of this assertion, Iqbal invoked, in his words, 'that immutable law of the Universe, which the Qur'an has enunciated in the simple but comprehensive verse: "God does not change the destiny of a people unless they change themselves."'[10]

Not everyone can be a poet. Of those that are, how many rise to the level where, in Goethe's image, they stand above the nations and feel a neighbouring people's woe?

Yet perhaps there is a role for everyone, including for the non-poet. That role is suggested in a letter that Iqbal wrote, upon learning of her father's death, to a German woman, a Miss Wegenast, whose first name is not provided in the source.

> Dear Miss Wegenast: I am extremely sorry to hear the sad news of your father's death; and though my letter must reach you a good many days after this sad event, yet neither time nor distance can make my sympathy with you in your bereavement any the less warm...
>
> *'Verily we are for God and to God we return.'* This is the sacred text that we recite when we hear the news of death. And I recited this verse over and over again on reading your painful letter. You remember that Goethe said in the moment of his death — 'More Light!' Death opens up the way to more light...
>
> I remember the time when I read Goethe's poems with you and I hope, you also remember those happy days when we were so near to each other —so much so that I spiritually share in your sorrows. Please write to me when you feel inclined to do so ... May God be with you. Yours ever, Mohammad Iqbal.[11]

The 'East' and 'West' of Iqbal's times have disappeared along with Goethe's 'East' and 'West', and along with any notions of 'East' and 'West' that Hafiz may have held. Whether Muslim or non-Muslim, the East now lives in the West, sometimes right next door to it.

In racial or religious composition, today's England, today's Germany and today's Europe are more mixed than they were twenty years ago, not to speak of Goethe's times. Yet proximity to a different race or faith has not produced either the bond or the richness that the German poet sought through his astonishing *Divan*.

The conversation he had with Hafiz, and the one that Iqbal had with him, is not being attempted today between residents living less than twenty yards apart in Europe's towns. Or in the towns and villages of America, Asia, Africa or Australasia.

Not everyone is a poet. Yet anyone may become a sympathiser, a listener, a sharer of sorrows and joys. A friend. Perhaps friendship is the heart of the *payams* – the messages – of Hafiz, Goethe and Iqbal.

The last-named was sustained by conversations in his Lahore home with friends (and fans) of different faiths. They were Sikh, Hindu, Christian and Muslim. As for Goethe, let me end with two quotations from the *Divan*:

And when people are divided in a mutual contempt, neither will acknowledge that they are striving for the same thing.[12]

Whoever knows himself and others will recognise this as well: Orient and Occident are no longer to be separated.[13]

Playing a Part: Imru' al-Qays in English

ROBYN CRESWELL

Before the delightful and occasionally dispiriting work of actual translation – the fussing over word choices, the tuning of voice, the arranging and rearranging of syntax – there is a more basic dilemma: not *how shall I translate* but *whom shall I translate*? There are few good rules for making this decision, but in 'An Essay on Translated Verse' (1684) the Earl of Roscommon offers some handy maxims:

> Examine how your humor is inclined,
> And which the ruling passion of your mind;
> Then seek a poet who your way does bend,
> And choose an author as you choose a friend:
> United by this sympathetic bond,
> You grow familiar, intimate, and fond;
> Your thoughts, your words, your styles, your souls agree,
> No longer his interpreter, but he.[1]

Goethe found such a friend in Hafiz, whose *ghazals* inspired the late verse of the *West-Östlicher Diwan*. Goethe did not translate Hafiz in any normal sense of the word, but he did claim an elective affinity with the fourteenth-century poet, whose antinomian cast of mind and worldly sensibility Goethe shared. In 'Unbegrenzt' [Unbounded], Goethe names Hafiz as both relation and rival, in lines any translator will recognise: Hafis, mit dir, mit dir allein / Will ich wetteifern! Lust und Pein / Sei uns, den Zwillingen, gemein!' (And, Hafiz, with you, with you alone, will I strive to compete! Let pleasure and pain be held in common for us, twins that we are!)[2]

The mystical union or spiritual sympathy evoked by Roscommon and Goethe is an ideal. In practice, translation is more like playing a part – both in the theatrical sense of role-playing, but also in the musical sense of playing only one piece (or part) of a larger whole. The elements of Hafiz that Goethe found sympathetic are not the same as those played up, for example, by Emerson, a serious translator of Hafiz who like Goethe first encountered the Persian poet in the German versions of Hammer-Purgstall. In 'Persian Poets', an essay published some forty years after the *West-Östlicher Divan*, Emerson praised Hafiz as a poet of epigraphic density and sudden, even jarring turns of thought – characteristic qualities of Emerson's own poems – and as a fellow disciple of 'that hardihood and self-equality of every sound nature'.[3] To somewhat overstate matters, Goethe's Hafiz is a soulmate and enlightened interlocutor, while for Emerson he is an epitome of flinty self-reliance.

If there is one classical Arab poet who has enjoyed something like a sympathetic bond with English language poets and translators, it is Imru' al-Qays, the pre-Islamic prince and author of one of the canonical *mu'allaqat*, or suspended odes. Imru' al-Qays's ode has been translated many times into English, but the most consequential version was arguably the first, by the philologist Sir William Jones, who published *The Moâllakât, or Seven Arabian Poems* in 1783.[4] In 'An Essay on the Poetry of Eastern Nations,' published a decade before these translations, Jones made a remarkable plea for the benefits, to scholars and poets alike, of a comparative literary education: 'If the principal writings of the Asiaticks, which are reposited in our publick libraries, were printed with the usual advantage of notes and illustrations, and if the languages of the Eastern nations were studied in our places of education . . . we should have a more extensive insight into the history of the human mind, we should be furnished with a new set of images and similitudes, and a number of excellent compositions would be brought to light, which future scholars might explain, and future poets might imitate.'[5]

Although the larger program of public education never happened, and although – Hafiz, Rumi, and Omar Khayyam aside – 'Eastern' poetry remains the terrain of specialists, Jones's English versions did solicit at least one important 'imitation'. For it was Jones's translations of the *mu'allaqat*, and his version of Imru' al-Qays in particular, which Alfred Lord

Tennyson used as a source for 'Locksley Hall' (1842), the long dramatic monologue that one contemporary judged to have 'had most influence on the minds of the young men of our day'.[6] 'Locksley Hall' is not a translation *sensu stricto* of Imru' al-Qays's poem, any more than Goethe's lyrics are translations of Hafiz, but the monologue can be read and heard as Tennyson's experiment in *playing the part* of the Arabic poet – a Victorian *mu'allaqa* that is fascinating precisely for those elements of the original it works up and those it sets aside.

Tennyson's poem begins with a couplet that evokes the famous incipit ('*Qifa nabki*') of the Arabic poem: 'Comrades, leave me here a little, while as yet 'tis early morn: / Leave me here, and when you want me, sound upon the bugle-horn.' Rather than the abandoned campsite of the Bedouin poet, Tennyson's speaker has returned to his ancestral hall, where he recalls a romance with his cousin Amy. The body of 'Locksley Hall' is a bitter reminiscence of this failed relation (echoing Tennyson's own disillusionment with Rosa Baring), in which the speaker laments Amy's choice to marry another man, bewails his own lack of station, and imagines a series of substitute satisfactions – whether a life of action, or a colonial fantasy of sensual abundance. At the end of the poem, the speaker's 'comrades' – presumably fellow soldiers, about to sail abroad – sound the bugle-horn, and the poet calls a storm down upon his former abode:

Comes a vapour from the margin, blackening over heath and holt,
Cramming all the blast before it, in its breast a thunderbolt.

Let it fall on Locksley Hall, with rain or hail, or fire or snow;
For the mighty wind arises, roaring seaward, and I go.

Critics have shown how much 'Locksley Hall' owes to Imru' al-Qays's *qasida*. It is likely that its long eight-stress trochaic lines, most of them falling naturally into tetrameter hemistiches, are Tennyson's version of an 'oriental' metre, with its origins in August Tholuck's German translations of Persian poetry (mediated by the 'Eastern' poems of Tennyson's friend, Richard Chenevix Trench). The lament over the ruined manor, the night vigil spent staring at constellations and the final storm scene, are clear reminiscences of the Arabic poem, which also ends with a vividly described lightning storm. Another shared element is the turn or sonnet-like *volta* by which the poet attempts to dispel memories of Amy and face the future squarely: 'Wherefore should I care? / I myself must mix with action, lest I wither by despair.' Tennyson's poem is full of such moments of self-admonishment, which mimic the Arabic convention of the poet vowing to break his bonds with the beloved, renounce his passions, and regain his manly composure (*hilm*).

Reading Imru' al-Qays in Jones's translation, Tennyson would have encountered not only a new repertoire of figures and themes, but also a novel theory of poetry. Along with his prose versions of the poems, Jones wrote a pair of essays in which he argued against an Aristotelian, mimetic understanding of poetry and claimed that verse was 'originally no more than a strong and animated expression of the human passions.' (This emphasis on expression rather than representation was, according to the scholar M. H. Abrams, the first systematic explication of the lyric poetics we now associate with English Romanticism.[7]) Furthermore, Jones claimed that no poetry exhibited this passionate utterance in purer form than the ancient 'Oriental' traditions. In 'An Essay on the Poetry of Eastern Nations', Jones writes, 'As the *Arabians* are such admirers of *beauty,* and as they enjoy such ease and leisure, they must naturally be susceptible of *that passion*, which is the true spring and source of agreeable poetry; and we find, indeed, that *love* has a greater share in their poems than any other passion.'[8]

Whether or not Jones's generalisation is true, Imru' al-Qays's *mu'allaqa* is notable for the length of its amatory prelude – ancient critics credited him with being the inventor of the *nasib* – and for being a poem in which the speaker never renounces his ruling passion. Instead of cutting the bonds of love, he exclaims (in A. J. Arberry's version), 'Let the follies of other men forswear fond passion / my heart forswears not, nor will forget the love I bear you.'[9] The Arab poet is a figure of *amour fou*, a persona of unrepentant excess. Tennyson's speaker, by contrast, is one who turns away from the passions of youth – 'I am shamed through all my nature to have loved so slight a thing' – toward the sterner duties of Victorian manhood. There is some echo of this resolute maturity in other pre-Islamic poems, but it is arguably the very antithesis of Imru' al-Qays's ode.

Frederick Seidel has shown the most consistent as well as idiosyn-
cratic interest in the old Arabic poems of any American writer. In 'The
Stars above the Empty Quarter' (1998), he pays homage to Labid, the
seventh-century poet and author of another *mu'allaqa*, for his praise of
a camel. Seidel's own poetry is full of odes to the motorcycle, and here
the objects of praise are characteristically mixed up:

> A pre-Islamic Golden Ode lists
> The hundred qualities of a camel.
> Suavity, power, the beauty of its eyes.
> Its horn, its tires, its perfect bumpers, its perfect fenders.
> The way it turns left, the way it turns right.
> The great poet Labīd sings
> His Song of Songs about the one he loves.
> How long it can go without water and without God.[10]

In another poem, '"Sii Romantico, Seidel, Tanto Per Cambiare"', Seidel
borrowed the Arabic monorhyme to write a truly frightening, if also
antic portrait of sexual decline:

> Easy to deride
> The way he stayed alive to stay inside
> His women with his puffed-up pride.
> The pharmacy supplied
> The rising fire truck ladder that the fire did not provide.
> The toothless carnivore devoured Viagra and Finasteride.[11]

This is a grotesque, fin-de-siècle version of amorous excess – Gustav von
Aschenbach wolfing down rotten strawberries. Remarking on the poem
during an interview published in *The Paris Review*, Seidel describes his
formal choices in theatrical terms: 'By using monorhyme I've forced
the formal elements to become a character. They are insisting that you
pay attention to them. They are onstage with the other elements of the
poem.'[12] But the most fully realised of Seidel's pre-Islamic 'translations' is
called 'Mu'allaqa' (2008), a poem he dedicates to Imru' al-Qays.
     Seidel's *mu'allaqa* begins at the end, with a storm scene that combines

a baroque metaphor from the ancient odes, the apocalyptic trumpets of Revelations, and a mighty wind out of *The Wizard of Oz*:

> The elephant's trunk uncurling
> From the lightening flashes
> In the clouds was Marie Antoinette,
> As usual trumpeting.
> The greedy suction
> Was her tornado vacuuming across the golden Kansas flatness.[13]

The rest of the poem deliriously juggles the themes announced in this opening stanza, while constantly slipping new objects into the mix. The French aristocracy on the eve of Revolution are conflated with Gulf royals, who dream of purchasing Versailles and 'pay payola to Al Qaeda to stay away from Doha' (are the repetitions and internal rhymes a tribute to the Arabic monorhyme?). The jihadis become accomplices of the approaching storm, contemplating the end of the world from their 'bitter *banlieus*'. Meanwhile, the poet – who cheerfully affiliates himself with the doomed aristocrats – takes centre stage, a Parisian aesthete mixed with the hunter-poet of the Arabic *tardiyya*: 'I kept a rainbow as a pet and grandly / walked the rainbow on a leash. / I exercised it evenings with the cheetah.' Like the ancient tribal poets, Seidel's poet remembers his debauched days of yore ('I left my liver in the Cher. / I ate my heart out *en Berry*'), but the excesses of the past pale in comparison to those of the present. In his own version of the *rahil* – the middle portion of a conventional polythematic ode, in which the poet mounts his camel for a difficult trip through desert – Seidel's poet travels through a nightmarish version of the UAE ('I see a desert filled with derricks / Pumping up and down but never satisfied') and the new France of 'north African hipsters' whose *ennui* leads to imagined apocalypse. In the final lines of the poem, the poet enacts a high-camp condensation of the *qasida*'s argument:

> I stomp the campfire out and saddle up my loyal *Mayflower* –
> Who is swifter than a life is brief under the stars!
> My prize four-wheel-drive with liquid wraparound eyes!

We ski the roller-coaster ocean's up and down dunes.
We reach land at last and step on Plymouth Rock.

This is not a poem of the passions. To stomp on the campfire is glee-
fully to reject the pathos of the *nasib* in favor of an eternal American
present, in which Plymouth Rock, Dorothy and Toto's Kansas, and the
speaker's *now* are all contemporaneous – as are, in a familiar paradox
of translation, Imru' al-Qays and Frederick Seidel, the Old world and
the New. Whereas Tennyson's rewrite of the *qasida* emphasises the pivot
between then and now, between erotic melancholy and nineteenth-
century optimism ('Forward, forward, let us range, / Let the great world
spin forever down the ringing grooves of change'), Seidel's lyric exists
in a depthless here and now. While Tennyson's speaker is a 'character',
who works through his feelings and changes his mind over the course of
the poem, Seidel's speaker is a dandy or performance artist, who never
grows up (even if he does grow old) and skips from excess to excess.

In their respective *mu'allaqat*, Tennyson and Seidel play up different
parts of the Arab poet's persona and discover different potentials within
the ancient ode. There are, of course, many other parts still unexplored,
and not only in Imru' al-Qays. Angie Mlinko's translations of al-Shanfara
and Labid, which take a page from Ezra Pound, find an equivalent
antiquity for the Arabic poems in Old English hemistiches and their
own rhetoric of ruin and waste. James E. Montgomery's translations of
'Antarah ibn Shaddad, which borrow some of their archaic atmospheres
from Mlinko, have made 'the Lord of War' into a recognisably (Scottish)
English poet. It is through the work of translation that Persianate forms
like the *ghazal* and *ruba'i* have become nearly as native to English
language poetry as the sestina and sonnet (which were once upon a time
translated from the Italian); in this way, 'formal' English verse is kept in
a healthy state of self-estrangement. But as the poems of Tennyson and
Seidel suggest, the translation and transformation of ancient 'Eastern'
poetry can also help 'Western' poets think through and clarify the
questions of what it means to be a Victorian British, or a fin-de-siècle
American, often with surprising results. William Jones's contention that
a general education including 'the principal writings of the Asiaticks'
would provide 'a more extensive insight into the history of the human

mind', as well as 'a new set of images and similitudes', still carries con-
viction and force – perhaps even more force now, when knowledge of
'Asiatik' poetry remains slight even as our worlds are drawn closer and
closer together. Future readers and poets will uncover further novelties
in these old verses. The ancient Arabic poems are like the glance of
the beloved as evoked by Abu Nuwas, *Wahid fi-l-lafz, shatt al-maʿani*:
'Singular in expression, multiple in meanings.'

Hafiz and the Challenges of Translating Persian Poetry into English

NARGUESS FARZAD

Marianne Moore, the renowned modernist American poet who lived most of her life in New York, described the Brooklyn Bridge as 'a caged Circe of steel and stone',[1] comparing this iconic structure, which connects the boroughs of Brooklyn and Manhattan, to the goddess of wizardry and enchantment. According to Greek legend Circe was skilled in the magic of transfiguration, and she possessed the ability to communicate with the dead to foretell the future.

Perhaps this is a good starting definition for a literary translator: an illusionist with a dual command of expressiveness and intuition who magically transforms the 'metaphysical conceits' of a poet writing in his or her own language, into the appropriate yet pleasing expressions and metaphors of a foreign language, all the while ferrying across as many aspects of the style, idiom and tone of the original as possible.

The metaphor of the translator as bridge is also an appropriate and fitting description, even if it has become something of a cliché. The translator is expected to establish vital connections between islands of culture, ideas and visceral emotions, regardless of the differences in topography and principles of literary composition, especially in the classical period. For such a metaphorical and practical lyrical bridge to withstand the passage of time and stylistic challenges while satisfying the evolving expectations of users, it must be supported by abutments – translators as well as copy-editors who are familiar with cultural idiosyncrasies and traditions of both the source and target languages – who can navigate the incongruous linguistic features on either side of the divide.

The finest and most treasured bridges are not only functional and safe, but they enhance the aesthetics of the landscapes they connect. They entice those who travel back and forth from one bank to the other to linger mid-span, take in the characteristics of the scenery spread out before them, and marvel at the solidity and beauty of the connecting structure.

The translator – or, increasingly in the realm of poetry, the interpreter – arranges the bailment of the precious gift of the original poem, left with him or her on trust, to a new linguistic destination. A conscientious translator will reflect on the hazards and pitfalls of the process of transference but no matter how successful will not aim to steal the thunder of the poet nor place him or herself at the centre of the project. Even the most acclaimed poet-translators of classical Persian poetry into English, such as Edward Fitzgerald, Matthew Arnold, Ralph Waldo Emerson, and Coleman Barks, who are of equal standing in fame and recognition to the poets they have translated, do not usually set out to eclipse the poetic twin whose original work has added another string to the poet-translator's bow, and in the case of Fitzgerald or Barks propelled them to international prominence.

The burden of responsibility weighs heavily on the shoulders of the translator when a much-admired writer such as José Saramago, the Portuguese novelist and winner of 1998 Nobel Prize in Literature, declares that 'writers create national literatures with their language, but world literature is written by translators'.[2]

However, in an effort to alleviate the enormity of the translator's burden, Susan Bassnett, one of the architects of translation theory, offers encouragement and a can-do attitude. Bassnett who endorses the image of the translator as a bridge has described this often invisible tribe as 'agents who facilitate the crossing over of a boundary'.[3] Moreover, she has taken issue with Robert Frost's oft quoted remark that 'poetry is what gets lost in translation,[4] calling this a 'silly' assumption, as if poetry were 'some intangible, ineffable thing or presence or spirit, which although constructed in language cannot be transposed across languages'.[5] This comment prompted David Bellos, the British born translator, and director of Princeton University's Program in Translation and Intercultural Communication, to his agreement and further comment that 'everything is *effable*, and the untranslatable does not exist'.[6]

While I would like to agree with the optimism and conviction of Bassnett and Bellos, my experience at the coalface of translating classical and modern Persian poetry, albeit as an amateur, tells a different story. Those of us who translate alone and time and again turn to our well-thumbed dictionaries and thesauruses, and increasingly a wealth of online treasure troves, searching for that elusive polysemous word, or the target equivalent of that apt aphorism in the source language, in the hope that our opaque, insipid, and clunky translation will magically be transformed into eloquent verse that makes the reader gasp in ecstatic appreciation, do not always agree with the assertive conclusions of the grand theorists – there are many poems that do indeed get lost in translation.

An impossible hyperbole in a thirteenth-century Persian mystical ode, for example, which will have native speakers swooning over its beauty and pithiness, more often than not will refuse to bend into a sonorous, lucid, and reflective gem in English translation, thrilling the hearts of those who read it or hear it recited.

The tried and true, centuries-old solution to this dilemma is to bring together a skilled, talented linguist – with bilingual proficiency in the source and target languages – with a poet, to work side by side to produce the best translation of a poem. It is this collaboration that will allow a distant and unfamiliar concept from one culture and language to be revealed from a fresh perspective in the recipient language.

It is worth remembering, as we mark and celebrate the two hundredth anniversary of the publication of the *West-östlicher Divan*, that Goethe was a great advocate of 'communicative translation',[7] which he discussed extensively in the 'Notes and Essays' that accompany the *Divan*. The imperative of translation as seen by Goethe is that the 'exact contextual meaning of the original is rendered in such a way that both content and language are readily acceptable and comprehensible to the new readership'.[8] For Goethe, known as much for his commentary as for his verse, the 'approximation of the foreign and the native'[9] would facilitate the understanding of the original poem and 'the whole circle is thereby closed upon itself'.[10] Furthermore, introducing the poetry of the 'other' via translation can revitalise and revolutionise the traditions of the host poetry culture, as demonstrated in the example of George Chapman's early seventeenth-century translations of the *Iliad* and the *Odyssey* into English and their influence on the poetry of John Keats. Similarly, the translations of the lyrical odes as well as the *Spiritual Couplets* of Rumi into so many languages since the 1980s has made his spirituality a fixture in the Western cultural sphere; every December, just a week before Christmas, the ancient city of Konya becomes a place of pilgrimage for tens of thousands of Rumi devotees from all over the world. Series such as the Penguin Modern European Poets; or initiatives like 'Words without Borders' and Stephen Watts's *Mother Tongues*; and the Poetry Translation Centre, the brainchild of the late Sarah Maguire, poet and translator, have made access to the poetry of eastern Europe, Latin America, Asia, Africa, and the Middle East significantly more accessible.[11]

The first noteworthy English translation of a *ghazal* by Hafiz, entitled *A Persian Song*, published in 1771, was done by the orientalist-philologist William Jones. The format of this softly romantic and in parts titillating poem is stanzaic and in keeping with the poetic style of the time. Although this English version is charming, and the metrical rhymes are aurally pleasing, the liberties that Jones has taken with the original, such as altering historical tones and omitting significant names, including that of Hafiz himself, have riled many critics. The poem begins:

> Sweet maid, if thou wouldst charm my sight,
> And bid these arms thy neck infold;
> That rosy cheek, that lily hand,
> Would give thy poet more delight
> Than all Bocara's vaunted gold,
> Than all the gems of Samarcand.

A century after William Jones, Gertrude Bell's moving interpretations of a selection of *ghazals* of Hafiz set a new standard for Hafiz in English. Over the years others such as Walter Leaf, Ruben Levy, John Nott, Edward Palmer, Elizabeth Gray, Robert Bly, Peter Avery, Daniel Ladinsky and Dick Davis have taken up the gauntlet of reproducing in English what are by far some of the most difficult yet enchanting examples of strictly metrical, consonantal, rhyme-rich, sensual Persian poetry, thick with assonance, sibilance and alliteration.

In some translations every jot and tittle of the Persian lines are transferred into English, while a few are so slipshod that it is hard to identify the original version. Some of the translators named above are academically proficient in Persian, and some operate through collaboration with native or near native scholars of Persian, or 'informants' as labelled by Ladinsky. Some of their translations have left indelible impressions on readers; others have fallen short of critical expectations.

The roll-call of the English translators of Rumi and Hafiz, just two of the most revered classical poets of the Persian speaking world alone runs into hundreds of names. A quick glance at the list over a continuum of nearly three centuries shows a frenzy of activity in the years between 1771 and 1895. Yet, despite the quality and variety of the translations, interpretations and verses inspired by the original poems amassed over the centuries, a quintessential English translation of the *ghazals* of Hafiz that retains the sinuosity, freshness and poetic energy of the original without succumbing to acculturations and excessive use of florid registers and archaic vocabulary – one that will allow the reader to experience what Leonard Lewisohn, calls the '*erotico-mystical*' essence of Hafiz, and stand alone as an independent poem – remains conspicuous by its absence.

An imaginative new translation could have a similar impact on a new generation of Western poets and their perception of this enigmatic Persian master of mysteries as Joseph von Hammer-Purgstall's 1812 German translation had on Goethe, and through him on Emerson, Tennyson, Keats, Byron, Eliot and Pound.

No one would ever claim that this would be an easy task. The linguistic and cultural challenges are immense. Non-Persian speakers, or those who do not dwell in the Persianate cultural domains, will always find the excessively emotive aspects of classical Persian poetry taxing. Winding their way through a multilayer love poem, they will need to work out whether the gender-neutral beloved's rosy, flushed cheeks, the curls of musk-scented hair, lips moist with drops of wine, amorous eyes personified as predators, intoxicated with expectation but ready to hunt with bow of brows and lethal arrows of lashes, are the appealing features of an immortal, divine beloved residing in celestial heaven, or the seductive and tantalising devices of a mortal muse taunting the poet in a tavern.

Below are several translations of the opening lines of the popular

Ghazal 22 of the *Divan* of Hafiz, which begins by describing the hurried arrival of a vexed and intoxicated beloved checking up on a lover who seems to be fast asleep in his bed. The poem is imbued with mystical signals while composed in a lasciviously seductive tone. Herman Bicknell sets the scene in 1872:

> With ruffled locks, with sweat drops dripping, beaming with smiles
> Near midnight, in disarray, you come . . .

Then, in 1898, Walter Leaf offers:

> Wild of mien, chanting a love-song, cup in hand, locks disarrayed,
> Cheek flushed, wine-overcome, vesture awry, breast displayed.
> With a challenge in that eye's glance, with a love-charm on the lip,
> Came my love, sat by my bedside in the dim midnight shade . . .

Moving by more than a hundred years to the early twenty-first century, Peter Avery quite accurately chooses the pronoun 'he' for the beloved and translates the lines as:

> Tress awry, sweating, laughing-lipped, drunk,
> Shirt in shreds, lyric-lisping, wine-cup in hand,
>
> His eyes spoiling for a fight, lips complaining,
> In the middle of last night, he came and sat by my pillow.

But, a decade later, Dick Davis changes the beloved back to a 'she':

> Her hair hung loose, her dress was torn, her face perspired
> She smiled and sang love, with mischief in her eyes,
> And whispering in my ear, she drunkenly inquired:
> 'My ancient lover, can it be that you're asleep?'

American poet Robert Bly, also prefers to retain the romantic conventions:

> Her hair was still tangled, her mouth still drunk
> And laughing, her shoulders sweaty, the blouse
> Torn open, singing love songs, her hand holding a wine cup.
> Her eyes were looking for a drunken brawl,
> Her mouth full of jibes. She sat down
> Last night at midnight on my bed.

It is quite clear that there will be as many interpretations and variations of the opening lines of this *ghazal* as there are translators.

Other practical challenges that the translator of Persian poetry will face are issues of prosody and scansion. If the translator decides to retain a metrical element of rhythm in the English version, he will need to reconcile the use of stress, a common tool in English composition, with the strict dominance of lengths and numbers of syllables that inform Persian metres.

Absence of gender in Persian will also force the translator to stumble and hesitate before labelling the beloved as a he or a she. The Persian language uses double negatives and employs two terms to denote the affirmative 'yes', *baleh* or *chera*, similar to the French *oui* or *si*, respectively, whereby one is used specifically for confirmation and the other for contention or contradiction. Classical Persian poetry relishes exaggerations and extravagant statements, and has access to more adages, verbs, and nouns than English when it comes to expressing nuances of romance, separation, longing and grief, and the process of death. The Persian poetic voice has a disposition toward ambiguity and the connotative use of words, while English poetry is more at home with transparency and candour.

While I have primarily focused in this essay on the importance of continuing to translate the best of classical Persian poetry and specifically the lyrics of Hafiz into English, my preference is for a shift of focus to the translation of the twentieth- and twenty-first-century poetry of the Persian speaking world, from Tajikistan in Central Asia to Afghanistan and Iran.

The three poets selected for inclusion in the *New Divan* each represent a unique aspect of the nonlinear development of modern Persian poetry. Emerging from their different origins and preoccupied with social or personal concerns that have in part been imposed on them by circumstances, they each hold up a mirror to the realities of twenty-first century urban life, which accepts exile, migration, reduction of the family into nuclear units, long-distance romance, nostalgia, victimhood, self-censorship, and all manner of rejection as par for the course.

The poems by Hafez Mousavi, Reza Mohammadi and Fatemeh Shams shine a light on the depth and breadth of a body of poetic discourse that can hold its own not just with the best of its classical predecessors but also with the finest modernist movements across the world. It is the job of the translator to convey the strength, complexity, and beauty of their poems.

The relative ease of travel between East and West, and the quickened pace of the teaching of modern European languages in Iran from the 1950s onward, on the one hand, and the increasing number of foreign visitors to Iran and Central Asia combined with the expansion of academic centres that prioritise the teaching of languages and comparative study of world literatures on the other, have all contributed to the greater familiarity of each side with the contemporary literary output of the other. While the works of celebrated twentieth-century Iranian poets such as Nima Yushij, Forough Farrokhzad, Ahmad Shamlou, Nader Naderpour, Sohrab Sepehri, Simin Behbahani and Qeysar Aminpour, to name but a few, are available in English translation and accessible either in print or digital formats, there are vast inconsistencies in the quality of the translations and only a small percentage do justice to the poignancy, sardonic humour or *angst* that overflows in line after line of many of these poems. Additionally, there are also gaps in the range of the poets represented, especially from Central Asia.

Travelling in the other direction, it is just as important that Persian-speakers have access to good translations of the new trends in heterogeneous poetry of the English-speaking world, composed by award-winning new voices who break the mould.

From amongst the established British and Irish poets Persian readers need to experience the brilliance of Seamus Heaney's poems in fresh translations, to experience his control of language and use of imagery as he narrates the pathos of mankind, and the way he composes — to borrow from one of his poems — 'the music of what happens'.[12] Would that Persian readers could have access to good translations of Walt Whitman, Robert Frost and Dylan Thomas, too. I would also add to this list exciting contemporary voices such as those of Liz Lochhead, Benjamin Zephaniah, Kathleen Jamie, Imtiaz Dharker and Richard Blanco, who merge everyday vernaculars, astringent social and political observations, and snapshots of their natural environment to produce poems brimful of quirky lyricism, with brush strokes of irony alongside vibrant optimism.

The reignited conversation between the West and the East, through the collaboration of multilingual translators and poets, will bring to the fore each side's experimentation with descriptions of natural and urban settings, and the relationship between the citizen and authority, and will allow each a glimpse of how regional and multicultural aspects of the lives of poets from across the world are fused with the voices of their poetic personas.

In the fourteenth century, Hafiz of Shiraz wrote in a synaesthetic *ghazal*: 'I have seen no memento more enchanting than the echoes of discourse of love, enduring in this revolving Dome'[13] and just over two centuries later Shakespeare responded: 'And when love speaks, the voice of all the gods, makes heaven drowsy with harmony';[14] the remoteness of their respective periods of writing, the differences of their circumstances, simply vanish.

When Nick Laird was working collaboratively on translations of a selection of Reza Mohammadi's poems for the Poetry Translation Centre, he commented in a blog piece on the 'weird pleasure' of 'opening your mouth and finding someone else's voice coming out'[15] – proving that Circe's sorcery indeed does work.

The New Tasks of the Translator:
The *West-Eastern Divan* and the problematic legacy of translation theories from Goethe to Benjamin

STEFAN WEIDNER

Translated from the German by Charlotte Collins

The *West-Eastern Divan*,[1] more than any other of Goethe's works, is the fruit of a translation; indeed, it could be said that, in a way, the *Divan* is itself a higher form of translation, a *Nach-Dichtung* in the true sense of the word.[2] Goethe also addresses the subject of translation in the 'Notes and Essays' he appended to the *Divan* poems to explain their cultural-historical background. In Goethe's *Divan* we are therefore presented with fundamental structures for dealing with translated cultures, and the translated 'Orient' in particular, that still impact on us today and have also influenced my own work as a translator from the Arabic. A peculiar tension exists between these structures – i.e. translation practice, then and now – and considerations such as those pinpointed by Walter Benjamin with reference to Goethe in his 1923 essay 'The Task of the Translator'.[3]

Many of Goethe's works are indebted to his encounters and engagement with other literatures. The *West-Eastern Divan* is an exception in that in this instance the stimulus derived from a totally different cultural context and was mediated by a translation from a language which Goethe – a few Arabic handwriting exercises notwithstanding – had not mastered, unlike the other languages whose literatures inspired him: French, Italian, English, Latin and Greek. When Goethe encountered Hafiz in Hammer-Purgstall's 1812 translation[4] and became fascinated by him, he found himself in a situation familiar to most modern readers (and almost all Western readers when the literature in question is an Oriental one) when dealing with foreign-language literature, namely: having to rely on the translation. Thus it is only in his engagement with Hafiz that translation, in Goethe's work, acquires both the significance and the problematic aspect we so often encounter in translated literature today.[5]

With this in mind, it is no surprise that the 'Notes and Essays', and thus the *West-Eastern Divan* as a whole, conclude with a short essay on translation.[6] Walter Benjamin ranks it, alongside observations by Pannwitz, as 'the best comment on the theory of translation that has been published in Germany'.[7] In it, Goethe differentiates between three styles of translation: first 'a plain prose translation',[8] of which he cites Luther's Germanisation of the Bible as an outstanding example. Secondly, Goethe refers to 'parodistic' translation; the example he gives for this is Wieland's translations of Shakespeare. 'Parodistic' should not be understood here as satire. Instead it means 'a concern to transpose oneself into a foreign country but in fact only by adapting foreign notions to one's own particular perspective'.[9] Finally he identifies the kind of translation that seeks to 'make the translation identical to the original'.[10] For this Goethe's example is the translation of Homer into German hexameters by his contemporary Johann Heinrich Voss.

Although each of these translation paradigms has its own merits, for Goethe the 'final as well as the highest'[11] is none other than the method of translation that renders it 'identical to the original' – not although but *because* in so doing the translator 'more or less abandons the originality of his own nation; and so a third element comes into being', through which, according to Goethe, the German is enriched and extended and 'versatility appeared among the Germans'.[12]

Benjamin borrows this approach to translation, writing:

> Therefore, it is not the highest praise of a translation, particularly in the age of its origin, to say that it reads as if it had originally been written in that language. [. . .] A real translation is transparent; it does not cover the original, does not block its light, but allows the pure language, as though reinforced by its own medium, to shine upon the original all the more fully. This may be achieved, above all, by a literal rendering of the syntax . . .[13]

Translation theories such as these raise a number of questions that require us, the translators of today, to adopt a position. As far as the questions themselves are concerned, the first that needs to be addressed is where the *West-Eastern Divan,* and the Hammer-Purgstall translation that inspired it, should be located within the framework of Goethe's and Benjamin's translation theories. The next thing we must do is ask ourselves what attitude we intend to take towards them, i.e. how do we want to translate today, especially when the material in question is supposedly 'culturally foreign'? Finally, we must examine whether the theories put forward are in fact applicable, i.e. whether they are borne out by translation praxis.

Goethe does not clearly state into which of his three paradigms he would classify Hammer-Purgstall's translation of Hafiz, but he would *like* to classify it into the third. He writes, cautiously: 'Von Hammer's works for the most part show a similar approach [*i.e. the manner of the third style of translation – SW*] to Oriental masterpieces. His approximation of their outer form is especially commendable.'[14]

However, Hammer-Purgstall is actually an excellent example of the second, parodistic style of translation. As far as form is concerned – the way he deals with the rhyme, for example – his approximation to Hafiz is extremely tentative. Whereas the original consistently uses the monorhyme – i.e. where each line of the poem ends with exactly the same rhyme – typical of classical Oriental poetry, Hammer's versions are predominantly written in unrhymed couplets or quatrains. Admittedly, we do already find occasional strophes consisting of only two lines, the two of them ending with the same word, serving as a substitute for the monorhyme.[15] However, Goethe's description of a style of translation that seeks to be identical to the original certainly does not pertain here:

> A translation which tries to identify with the original comes close to an interlinear version in the end; it makes an understanding of the original much easier. We are led to the fundamental text – indeed, we are driven to it – and so at last the entire circle within which the approximation of the foreign and the domestic, the known and the unknown move is drawn to a close.[16]

It must have been obvious to Goethe that Hammer's Hafiz translation does not correspond to these ideas and does not even tend towards an 'interlinear version'; however, he passes over this without comment. I suspect the reason is that, in a way, Goethe saw the *West-Eastern Divan* itself – i.e. his own poems – as a work that, according to the third translation variant, 'more or less abandons the originality of his own nation', thereby allowing something greater to come into being 'for which the public must gradually develop a taste'.[17]

In this context, Goethe notes that Voss's translation of Homer 'couldn't please the public at first but then bit by bit it learned to hear his new approach [to translation] and to feel comfortable with it'.[18] As he writes at the beginning of the 'Notes and Essays', Goethe feared the same fate might befall his *Divan*.[19] He hoped that this clarification would help 'readers who have little or no familiarity with the East [to] gain a more immediate understanding'.[20] He saw himself 'as a traveller for whom it is praise enough if he adapts comfortably and sympathetically to foreign ways, both aspiring to make other forms of expression his own and understanding how to enter into and assume other ways of thinking, other customs'.[21]

Thus the lyrical 'I' seeks to identify with the foreign world, and the traveller is essentially a personification of the *Nach-Dichter*. At the same time, however, Goethe knows that in his case this identification 'succeeds in this only to a certain degree'[22] and that he must also simultaneously assume 'the role of the merchant who spreads out his wares attractively and strives in various ways to make them appealing', in order 'that what the traveller brings back may all the more swiftly give pleasure to his compatriots'.[23] This ambiguity in Goethe's self-conception – as, on the one hand, the traveller who assimilates foreign customs, and on the other as the merchant who wants to make them pleasing to the public, to sell them, and who therefore has to make them less foreign – explains the peculiar dual nature of the *Divan*, as both a volume of poetry inspired by a foreign literature and a treatise that seeks to familiarise people with the literature of the Orient. Goethe, we may conclude, was perfectly aware that neither Oriental literature in German translation nor the *Nach-Dichtung* it inspires, such as the *Divan*, has any chance of finding readers and being appreciated by anyone other than specialists if it is offered up completely unmediated simply for what it is. In other words: as far as the Orient is concerned, Goethe's (and later Benjamin's) ideal of '[seeking] to make the translation identical to the original' does not appear to be a very promising undertaking, and neither Hammer-Purgstall nor Goethe seriously attempted it.

The reason for this is easily apparent. Voss's translation of Homer was well received (albeit, as Goethe comments, only after some time) because Homer was part of the Occidental educational canon. To stick with Goethe's metaphor of the *Nach-Dichter* as a travelling salesman, this meant that the 'goods' required no further marketing. Rather, because Voss's translation appeared to be closer to Homer than the other translations, Voss's version could be sold as the true, more authentic Homer – indeed, almost as the original itself. The same is true of the translators Benjamin lists as model exponents of the desirable style of translation that produces work identical to the original: 'Luther, Voss, Hölderlin, and [Stefan] George have extended the boundaries of the German language.'[24] However, the texts these translators translated in the manner described were all already part of the canon: Luther translated the Bible, Voss Homer, Hölderlin Pindar and Sophocles, while George translated Dante. In none of these cases was it necessary to familiarise people with the author, explain the cultural context, or answer the question of why they should be translated.

The opposite is true of Hafiz and other 'Oriental' authors when they are translated into European languages. They must first be rendered accessible to the public. With this in mind, it is unsurprising that Hammer-Purgstall's translation, according to Goethe's taxonomy, falls into the second, 'parodistic' category. Something similar can be said of Goethe's *Divan* poems themselves: to use Goethe's own (idiosyncratic) terminology, they are a 'parody' once removed – a parody of Hammer-Purgstall's (Hafiz) parody. However, this means nothing more than that neither Goethe's authorial nor Hammer-Purgstall's translation praxis corresponded to the ideal of translation and *Nach-Dichtung* postulated by Goethe and endorsed by Benjamin.

Nevertheless, in the nineteenth century it was precisely this thing at which neither Hammer nor Goethe managed to succeed, namely the translation and *Nach-Dichtung* of the literary Orient into something identical to the original, that was attempted by several German translators and poets, in particular Friedrich Rückert and August von Platen, who came closest to emulating the Oriental forms in the German language. Thanks to Rückert we have a German Hafiz who is, in the formal sense at least, much closer to the Persian Hafiz than Hammer-Purgstall's, and who imitates the monorhyme of Persian poetry.[25] It is also thanks to Rückert that we have a German Qur'an that rhymes, like the original.[26]

So would it not, after all, have been possible to '[turn] German into Hindi' (as formulated by Rudolf Pannwitz in the quotation by Benjamin[27]) – or, in our case, into Arabic or Persian? And shouldn't this ideal therefore still apply today? I must confess that I very much doubt it. It is my belief that the translation ideas propounded by Goethe and Rückert, Pannwitz and Benjamin have become questionable. They are certainly not suited to the translation of 'Oriental' poetry. Why?

First, it must be noted that these translation theories are not derived from praxis. Where attempts have been made to implement them – Rückert and Hölderlin are the best examples – the translations border on the unreadable, as Benjamin also observed when writing about Hölderlin's Sophocles translations: 'in them meaning plunges from abyss to abyss until it threatens to become lost in the bottomless depths of language'.[28] While Hölderlin's translations come (too) close to an interlinear version, Rückert's translations are afflicted by a different shortcoming. Versatile though the rhymes are, his language cannot shake off a nineteenth-century feel, and the obsessive, dogmatic use of rhyme gives the German a ponderous, laboured quality not found in any of the originals. It would not occur to a reader of Rückert's translations that the original texts were often set to music and sung, and that even ordinary and illiterate people know verses by Hafiz, Rumi or Ferdowsi by heart.

If we take this into account, the claim to identity or the ability authentically to 'turn' German into Hindi or Persian falls apart. *Changing* it into German is ultimately a selective process: one may retain only the formal aspects, for example, imitating rhyme and rhythm. The criterion for identity with the original remains extralinguistic. However ingenious the result may sound, it will seldom touch the heart as the originals do, and as more natural-sounding translations succeed in doing. Goethe and Hammer-Purgstall knew this, at least intuitively. They dispensed with *Nach-Dichtung* and the kind of translation that seeks to be identical, choosing instead the variant described by Goethe as 'parodistic'. Goethe's

Hafiz lives, not although but *because* he has evaded Goethe's own translation theory.

With translation that tries to identify with the original, it is not only the results that are often questionable; the ideology behind it is questionable, too. In Goethe this manifests itself in the assumption that languages and literatures follow a 'natural' course of development which is reflected in the different 'epochs' of translation and ultimately in a continuous assimilation of the various national literatures into each other, a process for which Goethe later coined the term 'world literature'.[29] Benjamin augments this notion to make of it a quasi-religious eschatology of translation: the translator is required to get close to the pure language – which remains, *per se*, inaccessible – by 'breaking' the boundaries of his own. Inherent in the idea of a 'pure language' is a vision of overcoming Babelesque linguistic diversity. If the translation 'breaks through decayed barriers of [the translator's] own language'[30] and, as Goethe put it, 'abandons the originality of his own nation', paradisiacal pre-Babel conditions come a little closer. Seen in this way, the 'task of the translator', as in the title of Benjamin's essay, is almost soteriological.

Worthy though these ideas may be, it is time they were discarded. They may once have promoted the reception of foreign, unfamiliar literatures. Today they impede it, or else harness translation to causes that have nothing whatsoever to do with literature, be they economic or, as with Walter Benjamin, political and philosophical (not to mention ideological, rooted in Hegel's dialectics).

Furthermore, the imitation of Oriental poetry in the interlinear style praised by Goethe, as well as by Benjamin and Pannwitz, does not break down barriers; it erects them. It banishes the Orient back to where it came from: the realm of the exotic. Like a colonial circus, it exhibits what is foreign and specifically *other* about the poetry – only in this way can German be 'turned into Hindi'. Where the translation really does make itself identical to that which is foreign, it invites not so much identification but differentiation, demarcation.

This is particularly true of new literature from the 'Orient'. The exoticising, alienating, interlinear translation envisaged by Goethe and Benjamin would be inappropriate here. Modern Arab or Iranian poetry is not alien and Oriental, as perhaps it may seem to the superficial observer. Rather, it must be seen as a branch or part of modern poetry as a whole, which is a worldwide phenomenon. The Arab and Iranian poets' responses to Goethe in this book are proof of this: surprising though they may be, they are in fact much closer to modern Western poetry than classical Arabic poetry or what Hamid Dabashi called 'Persian literary humanism',[31] meaning the tradition of which Hafiz is the best-known exponent.

Goethe references this Persian literary humanism but uses it as a disguise or role-play to write poems that, in literary-historical terms, can be classified as belonging to the Romantic or perhaps even Early Modern period. As such, it could even be said that, for literary Europe, the Orient was the midwife of the modern age. Meanwhile, Arab and Persian authors have been writing novels and modern poetry of their own for more than a century, and in the past twenty-five years this literature has increasingly been translated into European languages. A literary circle is being closed, and Goethe's words from the 'Nachlass' section of the *Divan* have proved true:

Whoever knows himself and others will recognise this as well:
Orient and Occident are no longer to be separated.[32]

It is therefore time finally to discover and appreciate the latent modernity of this supposedly other, foreign, Oriental literature – not least the latent modernity of Hafiz and of Persian literary humanism itself. The means for doing this are translations that do not lose themselves in technical acrobatics or seek the specifically poetic, interesting, special and valuable primarily in form (a very classical approach). Rather, they should bring out the spiritual and thus also poetic aspects of the original – translated texts whose form is not external, as often seems to be the case with rhyming translations, but in which form and substance merge into one.

As far as Arabic and Persian literature are concerned, many translations that succeed in doing this are now available to the English-speaking world.[33] However, the existing – mostly much older – German translations of Arabic and Persian poetry are predominantly stuck in the paradigms developed in the nineteenth century which I have criticised here. Newer, and novel, German translations of this poetry remain rare. I myself have translated primarily modern Arab poetry in the innovative, non-exoticising style described in this essay,[34] as well as one of the most famous volumes of medieval Islamic mystic poetry, *The Interpreter of Desires*[35] by Ibn 'Arabi (1165–1240). The response to these attempts was extremely positive, which ought to encourage the translator to continue in this vein. Ultimately, however, any such intention is dependent on the banal question of whether it can attract interested publishers, sufficient funding and enough readers. At present, at least for poetry, which is nearly always difficult to sell, the paradoxical answer given by most educated people still seems to be: what for? We already have Goethe!

Translating European Poetry into Arabic Culture

KADHIM J. HASSAN

Translated from the French by Lulu Norman

Ever since the founding of the famous *Bayt al-Hikma* (House of Wisdom) – an institution that specialised in the translation of Greek philosophical and medicinal texts into Arabic – in around 832, during the Al-Mamun caliphate, Arabic culture has been home to extensive translation activity, and at the centre of ethical and technical reflections on translation. Any relation to the text, style and thought of the Other has traditionally been characterised by great anxiety, in practice as much as in theory. After faltering beginnings, the desire of translators, philosophers and scholarly commentators not to distort or domesticate the text-as-object-of-translation, developed into concern and then into method.

On the threshold of the modern age, *Nahda*[1] translators were able to translate many more literary texts, whereas medieval Arabic culture had privileged scientific and philosophical translation. Little by little, as real translators appeared, as well as authors who made space in their practice for the critique of translations, good procedures were also being established. At the same time, there were cries of alarm, protesting the offences of some translators. Such cries reached a peak in the writing that Taha Hussein (1889–1973) – one of the fathers of modern Arabic literature, and himself the translator of Sophocles and Gide – devoted to criticising some of his contemporaries' methods. Condeming the excessive use of a 'sordid' and 'melodramatic' literary language on the one hand, and adaptive or truncated translations on the other, he called on translators to ensure they were reproducing what he called 'the exact image of the text'.[2] By exact image, he meant respect for the text's completeness, but also the safeguarding of the specificity of its language and its proper tone.

Translating poetry: the contributions of the Apollo group and Shi'r journal

We would have to wait until the end of the nineteenth century to witness the translation of any European poetry – or foreign poetry generally – into Arabic. For medieval Arabs, as for the *Nahda* pioneers, this was due to the rarity if not total absence of bilingual poets capable of translating what they read in other languages into an Arabic poetic form. One of the historians of literary translation in the Arabic language, Al-Munsif al-Jazzar, (who makes no mention of Suleiman al-Bustani and his verse translation of *The Iliad*, completed in 1900) saw the author of an Arabic version of Khayyam's Persian *Quatrains* (1912), Wadi al-Bustani, as the precursor of poetry translation into Arabic in the modern age.[3] But what was significant was that the chief method employed by the first Arabic translators of poetry was translation into verse. Al-Bustani's version of *The Iliad*, Lamartine's *The Lake*, translated by Nicholas Fayyad, and several translations of Khayyam's *Quatrains* are the best-known and most commonly cited examples. These verse translations, whose difficulties we will come back to, were surely motivated by their precocity: indeed it would be hard to imagine an immediate shift to free-verse or non-metric translation in a culture just beginning to discover poetry translation, which considered metre essential to poetry and still confused rhythm and metre, poetic writing and versification.

It would take the emergence of the *Apollo* group and the journal that bore its name to see poems in non-metric translations. Between September 1932 and December 1934, this journal would publish twenty-eight issues.[4] Inspired by Zaki Abu Shadi, who had established the *Apollo* school and edited the journal, a few poets and critics initiated a diverse approach. Their literary manifestos and theoretical contributions, as well as the new writing practices they preached, of which they themselves were exemplars, attest to an openness to different western literary trends and especially to the legacy of the Romantics. This creative and critical activity was complemented by non-metric translations that were the first of their kind. In the latter half of the twentieth century, other journals such as the Lebanese *Al-Adib* would pick up the baton. But it was the Lebanese journal *Shi'r* (Poetry), founded by Syrian-Lebanese poet Yusuf

al-Khal, which would elevate poetry translation to previously unimag-
ined heights.

This review's translators for the most part employed innovative
methods and techniques that were liberated from the yoke of metre:

1) They attempted modulation in order to generate a rhythmic tension
   within the line to match that of the original as closely as possible;
2) They made bold choices of vocabulary and syntax in an effort
   to coincide with the original, even at the cost of a few linguistic
   deviations or dispensations that would gradually become new
   writing procedures;
3) They used different registers of poetic speech and varied the tone,
   thus freeing the poem from a certain tonal solemnity that had
   attached to the majority of classical and even modern Arabic poetry.

With a few exceptions, the translation of poetry into Arabic would
thereafter follow the example of *Shi'r* journal. Translators of all genera-
tions, the majority themselves poets, now abandoned all concern for
metre and began to translate in rhythmic phrases similar to those of
European free verse with differing degrees of success. This has resulted
in a sizeable body of translations of European poetry. But truly successful
translations are extremely rare. When placed next to the original, even
translations that have become very popular, often by poets of repute, are
revealed to have major flaws and, sometimes, obvious errors. This proves
that further preparation is still required. But what is clearly lacking, too,
is any real theory of translation in general and of poetry in particular,
as well as a serious and methodological criticism of translations.

Problematic flaws and methods

Before commenting on what Arabic translations of foreign and particu-
larly European poetry have contributed, and their impact on the writing
of Arabic poetry, let us dwell briefly on their flaws, or the problems they
pose.

Versification: we have seen that the first translations of poetry respec-
ted the laws of Arabic metre. More recent translations have followed

suit. Rhyme is often a priority, as if rhyming itself constituted poetry. On the one hand this is to forget that the metres and rhyming systems of different poetic traditions do not overlap, even within sister languages, as in Romance languages (does the Alexandrine, for example, have the same history, configuration and resonances in all Romance languages?) And, on the other, that in translating metre, the conscious striving for verse and rhyme – which is flagrant folly, according to Borges[5] – attempts to reproduce what the poet had written in his metre instinctively. In this regard, a translation can be an over-translation, a rewriting of the text in another language rather than translation-as-writing.

Aestheticising the text: we must also note the suppression of elements considered ugly or shocking and the softening of obscenities or vulgar language, a diminution that Antoine Berman rightly condemns in his famous list of translators' inopportune interventions.[6] Like the 'anal ulcer' Rimbaud bestows on the consecrated, if not sacred, face of the Greek goddess in his poem *Venus anadyomene*, watered down by his Syrian translator Khalil Al-Khuri as a 'back ulcer'![7] Or this image from Ungaretti, '*La notte piu chiusa /lugubre tartaruga . . .*' ('The night more closed/ lugubrious tortoise . . . '[8]), prettified to the point of absurdity by Iraqi Saadi Yousef in '*Qamariyyatan, asyanatan*' ('Night . . . lunar, saddened).[9]

If we are missing the barely-concealed irony of a text, can we call it translating? Yet time and again in Palestinian Jabra Ibrahim Jabra's translation of *Hamlet*, this is what we encounter. To quote just one example, it is not clear why the translator distorts and dilutes the deliberately harsh words Hamlet addresses to his mother, believing she and his uncle have conspired to murder his father: 'Let the bloat king tempt you again to bed, / Pinch wanton on your cheek, call you his mouse'. Jabra Ibrahim Jabra translates the second part of this sentence as '*wa-yad'uki 'usfuratahu*' (and calls you his little bird[10])!

Removing repetition, the most egregious example of which occurs in translations of the Homeric epics. Homer was famously fond of repeating epithets in particular. In *The Odyssey*, Ulysses is 'the inventive', 'the divine', 'the cunning', 'the patient', 'the enduring', etc. These are not simply markers of meaning, helping us to establish characters, things and phenomena. They also, and more importantly, mark rhythm. According to the poet Philippe Jaccottet, author of a remarkable French translation of *The Odyssey*,[11] this repetition was a formal necessity, which is to say important for ritual elements. Jaccottet concludes: 'If we eliminate even some these formulas because their monotony no longer suits our taste, it is the very regularity of the epic that must be modified . . .'[12]

Archaicising poetic language. The most well-known examples can be found in the translation of Dante's *La Divina Commedia* by the Egyptian Hassan Uthman and Saint-John Perse's 'Étroits sont les vaisseaux' from *Amers* (1957) by Moroccan Mustapha al-Kasri.[13] The late lamented Jacqueline Risset, poet and author of a French translation of Dante's work, is very clear:[14] Dante's Italian was not old; it had just been born. To imagine that to translate it we must go back to ancient constructions in the target language is to confuse classicism with old-fashioned usage. The same is true for Perse, whose use of lofty language should not obscure its outright modernity.

Dismantling the rhythm (or rhythms) of the work. The most striking examples are again provided by Hassan Uthman in his translation of Dante and by Tunisian Mohsin bin-Hmida in his translation of Rimbaud's *Une saison en enfer*.[15] Bin-Hmida divides Rimbaud's prose poems arbitrarily into pseudo-verses and Uthman amalgamates Dante's famous *terza rima* into one long unbroken line, thus making this poetic song lose its essential surges and surprises.

The worst flaws, however, are represented by misunderstandings of language and culture. They appear in the work of translators who are not sufficiently versed in the source language or the work they are translating. Instructive examples can be found in Fuad Rifqa's translations. But even the celebrated Syrian-Lebanese poet, Adonis is not immune. The Tunisian critic Ali al-Luati[16] has identified a number of minsinterpretations in Adonis' translation of Saint-John Perse's poetic works. For example, in ' . . . monnaies jaunes, timbre pur . . . ', the word *timbre* is understood not in the sense of *sound* ('... the clear tinkle /of yellow coins...'), but of image or *postal stamp* (*damgha*). In 'Relations faites à l'Édile': 'relations' is translated as "'alaqat' ('relations' in the sense of *relationships*, not things related or said).

And we find a striking example of the lack of poetic culture and 'documentation' or 'erudition' relating to translated works – what Antoine

Berman in his above-mentioned work *La Traduction et la Lettre* calls 'translation scaffolding' – in the translation of Hölderlin's selected poems[17] by the Syrian poet Fuad Rifqa. In his translation notes, he defines Hyperion as being 'the name of the sun god' and Diotima as the 'symbol of love in Plato's *Symposium*'. Now every good reader of the German poet – elsewhere known as the author of a novel entitled *Hyperion or the Hermit in Greece* – knows that Hyperion is the pseudonym Hölderlin gave himself in some of his poems, just as he gave the name Diotima to his beloved Susette Gontard. Equally, Rifqa defines *Hesperien* as the 'symbol of the arrival of future gods'! But here Hölderlin is simply referring to Western land, which Germans call *Abendland* (Land of the sunset), an appellation the poet preferred in ancient Greek: *Hesperien*.

The impact of translation on Arabic poetry

The twentieth century saw poets' and Arabic readers' knowledge of European poetry deepening more rapidly from the 1940s on. Several factors came together to make this possible: the growing numbers of universities in the Arab world (the first, the University of Cairo, was founded in Egypt in 1908) and of European study trips; also greater access to foreign languages and the circulation of good literary journals which made space in their pages for translations of poetry. All these elements had the combined effect of advancing the art of translating poetry into Arabic and of increasing the impact of translations on the writing of Arab poets themselves.

In more recent years, some of the great occidental poetic oeuvres have found the right translators in Arabic. In the majority of cases, the translator demonstrates richness of vocabulary, powerful syntax, suppleness of rhythm and a profound grasp of the work's meanings, evident in their critical commentaries and explanatory notes which involve both interpretation and critical appreciation, over and above the work of translation. Translations by the Iraqi Sargon Boulus of Allen Ginsberg and W. S. Merwin, of Yves Bonnefoy by the Tunisian Mohamed Ben Salah, of Octavio Paz by another Tunisian, Mohamed Ali Al-Yousufi, or of various North American poets by the Palestinian Samer Abu Hawwash, provide good examples here.

To knowledge of the source language, good translations (of individual poems rather than complete oeuvres) will of course add to the Arabic language's capacity to offer refuge – *Un auberge du lointain* (An inn for the stranger), as the subtitle of Antoine Berman's excellent study, *La traduction et la lettre*, has it. In *After Babel*,[18] George Steiner lists the ways in which Hölderlin, in his translations of Pindar and Sophocles, has laboured to enlarge the expressive capacities of the German language, at the risk of scandalising many of his contemporaries. And we see similar creative daring in Pierre Klossowski's French translation of the *Aeneid*. Delaying meaning, anticipation, inversion, ellipses, neologisms, word contractions, etc., are operations that, like other great literary languages, Arabic – elaborated over fifteen centuries, bearer of a dizzying range of literature – is more than capable of performing. So the language has been able, with obvious success, to embrace the poetry of Eliot, Lorca, Char, Bonnefoy and many others.

The success of translations can be measured by their impact on poetry writing itself, and the influence of European poetry on Arabic poetry is clear. Of course, a misreading of Saint-John Perse's poetic work has led to a tendency towards list-making among some Arab poets, as well as a glorification of the poet's personality and world. But this is not always the case. Translations of surrealist poems, especially those of Jacques Prévert, have given us a more nuanced perception of reality as well as the option of using everyday language. Translations of Eliot's poetry have created a blend of poetry and philosophy, or meditative language. Translations of Lorca, Eluard and Neruda have given rise to a new lyricism, elaborated very differently, as well as a scathing irony, driven by Michaux, and the taste for aphorisms has gained enormously from translations of René Char. These are some of the fruits of translators' work, their contribution to the contemporary Arabic poem.

New poetic genres initiated by translation

From 1947 on, two Iraqi poets, Badr Shakir al-Sayyab and Nazik al-Malaika, soon followed by another, Abd al-Wahhab al-Bayati, in common with many poets from all over the Arab world, broke with the *qasida*, the classical Arabic poem subject to the dual law of two hemistiches and a single rhyme. They did this by proposing a new poetic form based on one verse of unequal length, a varying number of feet and varied rhymes, which they called 'free verse' (literally, *sh'ir hurr* or 'free poetry'). By radically altering Arabic verse in this way, these new poets were in fact calling for a total revision and complete overhaul. They have to some extent succeeded in prompting an entire culture (which had formed them) to change the way it conceived of the world, language and the writing of poetry.

That said, we should not forget the significant differences between Western and Arabic metres. Verses written in a Romance language tend to be syllabic. Arabic poetic metre is based on *feet* (*tafa'il* or *taf'ilat*), and is often compared to Greek and Latin metres. Free verse in the Romance languages uses variable *metres* and *lengths*. Despite bold experiments mixing different metres, by Sayyab in particular, Arabic free verse remains faithful to one metre, so his sole innovation was to vary the number of feet in a line.

A few years later, this free verse with a variable number of feet found itself alongside another kind of verse in Arabic, no longer haunted by feet and rhyming, and thus similar to European free verse. This verse largely owes its invention to translations of European poetry. Other poets, like the Lebanese Pierre Adib, had certainly taken tentative steps in that direction from the 1940s on, but it was Syrian Muhammad al-Maghut more than anyone who, in the pages of the *Shi'r* review, popularised the form and became its most famous practitioner. We now know that this autodidact poet's only language was Arabic and in many interviews he referred to adopting free or non-metric verse because of the influence of European poetry translations that were not in verse and did not rhyme. And it was almost at the same time, also prompted by European and especially French poetry and its translation that the Arabic prose poem emerged, written in a single block, following models of the form extant in other world poetry.

Of course there is no need to underline here the power and variety that modern Arabic poetry has accrued from the emergence of these three new poetic forms: Arabic free verse with a varying number of feet, non-metric Arabic free verse and finally the Arabic prose poem. But we do need to be aware and make clear that Arabic poetry has been enriched with new poetic forms and genres through an openness to European poetry, read in the original but also in translation; to this it owes the imaginative freedom and verbal strength that we find in its best examples.

NOTES ON THE POEMS

Khaled Mattawa: Easter Sunday, Rajab in Mid-Moon

p. 6   *Rajab*: The seventh month of the Muslim calendar and one of four 'holy months'. It was a month of fasting and atonement; more importantly, it was a 'month of peace' in which warfare was banned. The Prophet is said to have called it 'the month of God', claiming Sha'ban as his month and Ramadan as the 'month of my people'. According to tradition, Mohammad was conceived on the first night of Rajab; he is also said to have made his 'night journey' during the last days of that month.

Khidr: The figure of Khidr, mentioned in the Qu'ran, in sura 18 (though not by name), is a prophet in Islamic tradition. The name 'Khidr' (related to the word for 'green' in Arabic) led to his designation as 'the Green One'. Grass springs up about his feet in barren lands; he is the keeper of the spring of eternal life. He is sometimes depicted as a young man with a white beard, to emphasise both his everlasting youthfulness and his venerability.

p. 7   *Who long for death in flame*: See Goethe's *West-Eastern Divan*, translated and annotated by Eric Ormsby, The Book of the Poet, Poem 17 (London: Gingko, 2019).

Hafez Mousavi: The Name of that Sad Dove

p. 91   *bathing their baby*: 'If its gentle hands a new-born one/ Move, then straightway turn it tow'rd the sun' – from 'Parsi Nameh (The Book of the Parsi)', *West-Eastern Divan*.

God sparks!: 'Ode to Joy' by Schiller.

Baucis and Philemon: Goethe's *Faust*, Mephistopheles burns down Baucis and Philemon's hut.

Heine's muse: 'I only trust your eyes now, they're my heavenly lights' Heinrich Heine

Eternal Womanhood: Closing lines of Goethe's *Faust*.

Todesfuge: 'Death Fugue' by Paul Celan.

never turned white: Celan's mother died young in a Nazi concentration camp in 1943.

black milk of morning: 'Death Fugue' by Paul Celan.

whittle his flutes: 'Chorus of the Rescued' by Nelly Sachs.

p. 93   *whore, whose child*: 'To the Silenced' by Georg Trakl.

funeral shrouds: 'The Silesian Weavers' by Schiller.

those other fools: 'Questions' by Heinrich Heine.

the panther: 'The Panther' by Rilke.

a white elephant moves: 'The Carousel' by Rilke.

at the seaside: 'Young Lady at the Seaside' by Heinrich Heine.

The name of the sad dove: 'Earthly Verses' by Forough Farrokhzad.

Clara Janés: The Song of the One Who Pours the Wine

p. 94   *A word's a fan*: Goethe, 'Das Wort ist ein Fächer', *Diván oriental.occidental*. Poem 27, The Book of Hafiz, *West-Eastern Divan*, translated and annotated by Eric Ormsby (London: Gingko, 2019).

p. 96   *Nature, my one joy is to connect*: Goethe, 'Sei es mein einziges Glück, dich zu berühren, Natur!' (Let my only joy be to touch you, Nature!), *Epigramme* (Venedig 1790), n° 78.

NOTES ON THE ESSAYS

Sibylle Wentker

1   For this and all other references to Goethe's *Divan* in this article see Johann
     Wolfgang von Goethe, *West-Eastern Divan*, translated and annotated by Eric Ormsby
     (London: Gingko, 2019).

2   *To God belongs . . .*: Goethe, 'Talismans', The Book of the Poet, *West-Eastern Divan*.
     These famous lines from the *West-Eastern Divan* allude to Qur'an 2:142: 'East and
     West belong to God. He guides whomever He will to the right way.'

3   Hamid Tafazoli, *Der deutsche Persien-Diskurs* (Bielefeld: Aisthesis, 2007).

4   Johann Wolfgang von Goethe, *Sämtliche Werke, West-östlicher Divan*, 2 vols
     (Frankfurt am Main: Klassiker Verlag, 2010), Vol. 1. p. 727.

5   Hartmut Bobzin, 'Review: Der Diwan von Mohammad Schems ed-din Hafiz.
     [Nachdruck der Ausgabe Tübingen: Cotta 1812/13]' in *Zeitschrift der Deutschen
     Morgenländischen Gesellschaft*, 153/1 (2003), p. 236.

6   Joseph von Hammer-Purgstall, *Erinnerungen aus meinem Leben*, Typoskript,
     Archiv der Österreichischen Akademie der Wissenschaften, Wien, Nachlass
     Hammer-Purgstall, Book 3, Cahier 3, p. 17.

7   Joseph von Hammer, *Der Diwan des Mohammed Schemsed din Hafiz, zum erstenmal
     ganz übersetzt*, 2 vols (Stuttgart: Cotta 1812–13), p. iii.

8   William Jones, *A Grammar of the Persian Language* (London: W. and J. Richardson,
     1771) and *Dissertation sur la littérature orientale* (London: P. Elmsly & Richardson &
     Urquhart, 1771) both appeared in the same year, 1771.

9   Encyclopaedia Iranica, XV, s.v. William Jones, pp. 5-11 (Michael J. Franklin).

10   Encyclopaedia Iranica, XI, s.v. Hafez i, pp. 461–5 (Ehsan Yarshater).

11   Encyclopaedia Iranica, XI, s.v. Hafez i, p. 463 (Ehsan Yarshater).

12   Encyclopaedia Iranica, XI, s.v. Hafez i, p. 464 (Ehsan Yarshater).

13   Annemarie Schimmel, 'The Genius of Shiraz: Sa'di and Hāfez' in Ehsan Yarshater'
     (ed.), *Persian Literature* (New York: Bibliotheca Persica, 1988), pp. 219–21.

14   John D. Yohannan 'Persian Literature in Translation' in Ehsan Yarshater, *Persian
     Literature*. New York: Bibliotheca Persica, 1988), p. 479.

15   'Open Secret', Book of Hafiz, *West-Eastern Divan*, p. 59.

16   Annemarie Schimmel, 'The Genius of Shiraz: Sa'di and Hāfez' in Ehsan Yarshater
     (ed.), *Persian Literature* (New York: Bibliotheca Persica, 1988), p. 220.

17   Ingeborg Solbrig, *Hammer-Purgstall und Goethe. ,Dem Zaubermeister sein Werkzeug'*
     (Bern: Lang, 1973), p. 102.

18   Joseph von Hammer: *Geschichte der schönen Redekünste Persiens mit einer Blüthenlese
     aus zweyhundert persischen Dichtern* (Wien: Heubner und Volke, 1818), p. 262.

19   *Encyclopaedia Iranica*, online edition 2016. Hamid. Algar, Bosnia and Herzegovina;
     http://www.iranicaonline.org/articles/bosnia-and-herzegovina.

20   Herman Brockhaus (ed.): *Die Lieder des Hafiz, persisch mit dem Commentare des Sudi*,
     3 vols (Leipzig: Brockhaus, 1854–60), I, p. vi.

21   Hammer 1812/13, p. IV.

22 Nima Mina, *Anmerkungen zur Joseph von Hammer-Purgstalls Hafiz-Übersetzung* (Graz: Medienfabrik Graz, 2007), p. 12.

23 Ibid., p. 101.

24 Ibid., pp. 104–5.

25 Ibid., p. 107.

26 Walter Höflechner and Alexandra Wagner (eds.), *Joseph von Hammer-Purgstall. Erinnerungen und Briefe*, 3 vols (Graz: Publisher, 2011), Vol. 2, p. 1406–7. (http://gams.uni-graz.at/context:hp)

27 Hammer-Purgstall, *Erinnerungen*, Book 30, Cahier 3, p. 22.

Rajmohan Gandhi

1 Obama to one of his speechwriters, Ben Rhodes, quoted in an article by George Packer in the *New Yorker*, 18 June 2018.

2 Johann Wolfgang von Goethe, Poem 95, The Book of Wisdom, *West-Eastern Divan*, translated and annotated by Eric Ormsby (London: Gingko, 2019), p. 165.

3 Introduction by Martin Bidney in Goethe, *West-East Divan* (New York: State University of New York Press, 2010), p. xxxi.

4 In Sheikh Muhammad Ikram, *Modern Muslim India and the Birth of Pakistan* (Lahore: Institute of Islamic Culture, undated), p. 171.

5 Translated by M. Hadi Hussain [add publication details if available]. http://www.allamaiqbal.com/works/poetry/persian/payam/translation/index.htm

6 *The First Part of Goethe's Faust*, tr. by John Anster (London: George Routledge & Sons, 1887), p. 188.

7 Oskar Loerke, 'Einleitung' to Goethe, *West-Östlicher Divan*, ed. Oskar Loerke (Berlin: S. Fischer Verlag, 1925), quoted in the introduction by Martin Bidney to Goethe, *West-East Divan* (New York: State University of New York Press, 2010), p. xxxiii.

8 Johann Wolfgang von Goethe, *Conversations with Eckerman* (sup. Sunday, 7 March 1814).

9 Ibid.

10 Iqbal's words are from Anil Bhatti, 'Iqbal and Goethe: A Note', *Yearbook of the Goethe Society of India*, 1999–2000, S. 184–201, p. 10. http://www.goethezeitportal.de/db/wiss/goethe/bhatti_iqbal.pdf

11 Date of letter not given in the source. See 'Muhammad Iqbal and Germany' by M. A. H. Hobohm in http://www.iqbal.com.pk/944-allama-iqbal-studies/scholarly articles/1633-muhammad-iqbal-and-germany

12 Johann Wolfgang von Goethe, Poem 69, The Book of Ill-Humour, *West-Eastern Divan*, translated by Eric Ormsby (London: Gingko, 2019).

13 Johann Wolfgang von Goethe, Poem 241, Appendix, *West-Eastern Divan*, translated by Eric Ormsby (London: Gingko, 2019), p. 577.

Robyn Creswell

1 'Earl of Roscommon, 'An Essay on Translated Verse' in *Augustan Critical Writing*, ed. David Womersley (London: Penguin, 1977), p. 111, ll. 93–100.

2 Johann Wolfgang von Goethe, 'Unbounded', Poem 23, The Book of Hafiz, *West-Eastern Divan*, translated and annotated by Eric Ormsby (London: Gingko, 2019), p. 55.

3   Ralph Waldo Emerson, 'Persian Poetry' in *The Complete Works of Ralph Waldo Emerson*, ed. Edward Waldo Emerson vol. 8 [Letters and Social Aims] (Boston: Houghton Mifflin, 1904) p. 247.

4   Sir William Jones, *The Collected Works of Sir William Jones*, vol. 10 (London: J. Stockdale, 1807).

5   Ibid., pp. 359–60.

6   Charles Kingsley, *Literary and General Lectures and Essays* (London: Macmillan, 1890), p. 114.

7   M. H. Abrams, *The Mirror and the Lamp: Romantic Theory and the Critical Tradition* (Oxford: Oxford University Press, 1953), p. 87.

8   Jones, *The Collected Works* , vol. 10, p. 338.

9   A. J. Arberry, *The Seven Odes* (London: George Allen & Unwin, 1957), p. 63.

10   Frederick Seidel, *Poems 1959–2009* (New York: Farrar, Straus & Giroux, 2009), p. 244.

11   Ibid., p. 11.

12   'The Art of Poetry No. 95', *The Paris Review*, 190 (Fall 2009), p. 165.

13   Seidel, *Poems*, p. 27.

Narguess Farzad

1   Marianne Moore, 'Granite and Steel' in *The Complete Poems of Marianne Moore* (London: Penguin Books, 1994).

2   José de Sousa Saramago reportedly made the statement in May 2003 during a speech at the Fourth Latin American Conference on Translation and Interpretation in Buenos Aries. ATA Chronicle 32, no. 6 (June 2003), at http://www.atanet.org/chronicle-online/wp-content/uploads/203-June.pdf.

3   Susan Basnett and André Lefevre, eds., *Constructing Cultures: Essays on Literary Translation* (Bristol: Multilingual Matters, 1998).

4   Robert Frost, 'The Figure a Poem Makes', preface to *Collected Poems* (New York: Halcyon House, 1939).

5   Susan Basnett and Lefevre, p. 57.

6   David Bellos, *Is That a Fish in Your Ear?* (London: Penguin Books, 2012), p. 156.

7   Peter Newmark, *Approaches to Translation* (Oxford: Pergamon Press, 1981), p. 41.

8   Peter Newmark, *A Textbook of Translation* (Hemel Hempsted: Prentice Hall, 1988), p. 41.

9   Johann Wolfgang von Goethe, 'The Natural forms of Poetry' in 'Notes and Essays', *West-Eastern Divan*, translated and annotated by Eric Ormsby (London: Gingko, 2019), p. 419.

10   Ibid.

11   See: https://www.wordswithoutborders.org; Stephen Watts, Daniel Weissbort and Norma Rinsler, eds, *Mother Tongues* (London: MPT Books, 2001); http://www.poetrytranslation.org.

12   Seamus Heaney, *Field Work* (London: Faber, 1976), p.56.

13   Hafiz, Ghazal no. 175, Khānlari edition of the *Divan of Hafiz*, 1983.

14   William Shakespeare, *Love's Labours Lost*, Act IV, Scene 3.

15   Nick Laird, Nick Laird, 'On Translating Reza Mohammadi', http://www.poetrytranslation.org/articles/nick-laird-on-translating-reza-mohammadi

Stefan Weidner

1   Johann Wolfgang von Goethe, *West-Eastern Divan*, translated and annotated by Eric Ormsby (London: Gingko, 2019), hereafter referred to as the *Divan*.

2   *Translator's note*: Breaking up the German compound word into 'Nach-Dichtung', as here, suggests a literal reading, i.e. 'poetry after [an original]'. A *Nachdichtung* is a version, free rendering or reworking inspired by an earlier work. Cf. *Nachdichter*, the author of such a version, and the verb *nachdichten*.

3   In Walter Benjamin, *Selected Writings*, ed. Marcus Bullock and Michael W. Jennings (Cambridge, Mass: Belknap, Harvard University Press, 1996), Vol. 1, p. 253 ff.

4   Mohamed Schendsed-din Hafis, *Der Diwan*, translated into German from the Persian by Joseph von Hammer-Purgstall (Munich: Süddeutsche Zeitung Edition/Bibliotheca Anna Amalie, 2007).

5   Emily Apter has written extensively about this problematic aspect in *Against World Literature: On the Politics of Untranslatability* (New York: Verso, 2013), and in *The Translation Zone: A New Comparative Literature* (Princeton: Princeton UP, 2006).

6   *Divan*, 'Notes and Essays', pp. 496–500.

7   Benjamin, p. 261.

8   Goethe, *Divan*, p. 496.

9   Karl Richter, in his commentary on the *West-Eastern Divan* in: *Johann Wolfgang Goethe, Sämtliche Werke nach Epochen seines Schaffens*, Munich edition, Vol. 11.1.2, (Hanser Verlag: Munich, 1998), p. 835.

10   Goethe, *Divan*, p. 498

11   Ibid.

12   Ibid.

13   Benjamin, p. 260

14   Goethe, *Divan*, p. 498.

15   e.g. numbers CVI–CIX in the first edition used by Goethe (identical to the edition referenced in footnote 4).

16   Goethe, *Divan*, p. 500.

17   Goethe, *Divan*, p. 498.

18   Ibid.

19   The *Divan* was indeed ignored by the general public. It was still possible to obtain a first edition from the publisher, Cotta, in the early twentieth century.

20   Goethe, *Divan*, p. 345.

21   Ibid.

22   Goethe, *Divan*, p. 346.

23   Ibid.

24   Benjamin, p. 261.

28   Hafis, *Ghaselen*, translated into German by Friedrich Rückert (Zürich: Manesse, 1988).

26   *Der Koran*, translated into German by Friedrich Rückert, ed. Hartmut Bobzin (Würzburg: Ergon, 2001).

27   Benjamin, pp. 261–2. The German word used by Pannwitz, 'verindischen' (lit. to make Indian, translated here, by Bullock and Jennings, as 'to turn German into Hindi'), appears in a quotation from *Die Krisis der europäischen Kultur* (1917). Interestingly, it occurs in the context of a discussion of Karl Eugen Neumann's translation of the

teachings of Buddha (cf. p. 191 in the 1947 edition published by Verlag Hans Carl), but Benjamin does not mention this.

28 Benjamin, p. 262. In his *Lectures on the History of Literature Ancient and Modern, Part Two: 1802–1803*, Wilhelm Schlegel had already remarked with regard to specifically German attempts to imitate foreign forms of poetry that some people might 'at least have doubts about the possible popularity of such poems'. (Quoted in *Geschichte der klassischen Literatur*, Stuttgart 1884, p. 11.)

29 Conversations with Eckermann, 198, 31.1.1827: 'National literature does not mean much at present, it is time for the era of world literature and everybody must endeavour to accelerate this epoch.'

30 Benjamin, p. 261.

31 Cf. Hamid Dabashi, *The World of Persian Literary Humanism* (Cambridge, Mass.: Harvard UP, 2012).

32 Goethe, *Divan*. Appendix, Poem 241, p. 577. Interestingly, as Hendrik Birus speculates, this poem was probably only written several years after the composition of the *Divan*, namely in 1826. (See p. 1777 of the Deutscher Klassiker Verlag edition of Goethe's *West-östlicher Divan*, Parts 1 and 2 [Frankfurt 1994], edited and with a commentary by Hendrik Birus.)

33 I will mention here only the well-known Rumi translations of Coleman Barks and John Moyne in *The Essential Rumi* (New Jersey: Castle Books, 1997) and the extremely successful Hafiz *Nachdichtung* by Robert Bly and Leonard Lewisohn, *The Angels Knocking on the Tavern Door: Thirty Poems of Hafez* (New York: Harper Collins, 2008).

34 e.g. *Die Farbe der Ferne. Moderner arabischer Dichtung*, translated and edited by Stefan Weidner (Munich: C. H. Beck, 2000).

35 Ibn 'Arabi, *Der Übersetzer der Sehnsüchte*. Poems. Edited and translated by Stefan Weidner (Salzburg: Jung und Jung, 2016).

Kadhim J. Hassan

1 *Nahda* (lit. awakening) is the name given to the cultural and political Arab renaissance from the nineteenth century onwards.

2 Cf. in particular Taha Hussein, *Mustaqbal al-thaqafa fi misr* (The Future of Culture in Egypt), 1938, and *Hafiz wa Chawqi* (Hafiz and Chawqi), works often reissued in Egypt by Hay'at al-thaqafa al-'amma (Egypt).

3 Munsif al-Jazzar, 'Al Tarjama al-Adabiyya' (Literary translation), in *Al-tarjama wa-nazariyyatuha* (The translation and its theories), collective work (Carthage: Bayt al-Hikma editions, 1989).

4 For a wider discussion of the points that follow, see my *La Part de l'Étranger – la traduction de la poésie dans la culture arabe* (Arles-Paris: Editions Actes Sud/Sindbad, 2007).

5 George Steiner, *After Babel – Aspects of Language and Translation* (Oxford: Oxford University Press, 1975), French translation: G. Steiner, *Après Babel : Une poétique du dire et de la traduction*, traduit par Lucienne Lotringer (Paris: Éditions Armand Colin), 1978, p. 78.

6 Cf. A. Berman, *La traduction et la lettre ou l'auberge du lointain* (Paris: Seuil, 1999). The examples in these paragraphs are all taken from Arabic translations that enjoy a

certain renown, since no new translations of the same works have appeared, offering new readings. For more details see again Kadhim J. Hassan, *La Part de l'Étranger – la traduction de la poésie dans la culture arabe*, op. cit.

7   A. Rimbaud, *Hayatuhu wa-shir'ruh*, (Rimbaud, His Life and His Poetry), translated by Khalil al Khuri (Baghdad: Maktabat at-Tahrir editions, 1st edition 1978, 3rd edition 1985), p. 94.

8   G. Ungaretti, *Vie d'un homme, Poésie 1914–1970*, French translation by Philippe Jaccottet, Pierre Jean Jouve, Jean Lescure and others, preface by Philippe Jaccottet (Paris: Poésie/Gallimard, 1969 (1st edition, Éditions de Minuit, 1954)), p. 31.

9   G. Ungaretti, *Shi'r mutarjam* (Ungaretti, translated poems), translated by Saadi Youssef (Beirut: Ibn Rushd editions, 1981), p. 19.

10 William Shakespeare, *Hamlet*, translated into Arabic by Jabra Ibrahim Jabra (Beirut: Editions Al-mu'assasa al-arabiyya li-l-dirasat wa-l-nashr, 1960), p. 146.

11 *L'Odyssée, Homère*, French translation by Philippe Jaccottet (Paris: Editions François Maspero, La Découverte, 1982 (1st edition by the Club Français du Livre), 1955).

12 *Ibid.*, postface, p.104.

13 S-J Perse, *Al fulk al-dayyiqa*, translated into Arabic by Mustafa al-Kasri (Tunis, Al-Dar al-tunissiyya li-l-nashr, 1973).

14 Cf Jacqueline Risset, *Dante écrivain* (Paris: Seuil, coll. Fiction et Cie, 1982).

15 Artur Rambu [Arthur Rimbaud], *Fasl fî Jahannam* (*A Season in Hell*), trans. Muhsin Ben Hamida (Tunis: al-Sharika al-Tunisiyya li-t-tawzi', 1987).

16 Ali al-Luati, 'Jinayat Adonis 'ala Saint-John Perse' in *Saint John Perse, Anabaz, Manfa wa-qasa'id ukhra* (*Anabase, Exile and other poems*) (Tunis: Editions Al-Dar al-'arabiyya li-l-kitab, 1985).

17 Hölderlin, *Mukhtarat min shirih* (selection of poetry), translated into Arabic by Fuad Rifqa, (Beirut: Editions Al-Ahliyya li-l-nashr wa-l-tawzi', 1974).

18 George Steiner, *After Babel*, op. cit.

EDITORS' NOTE

To create this lyrical dialogue, we commissioned twenty-four poets to write poems in response to the themes of the twelve books of Goethe's original *Divan*. The twelve poets from the 'East' write in Arabic, Persian and Turkish, while the twelve from the 'West' write in English, French, German, Italian, Portuguese, Russian, Slovenian and Spanish. Our aim was to find poets keen to engage with Goethe's original, but also with an awareness of the divided times in which we live. It would have been possible to go only to poets already interested in 'East' and 'West', but what we also wanted to do was to encourage poets established in their own cultures to engage with poetry and culture not their own, to open themselves up to new influences and new experiences.

This matters because poetry thrives and develops by cross-fertilisation. Thinking only of English-language poets, it is difficult to imagine how Ezra Pound and T.S. Eliot could have written their modernist poetry without a deep immersion in the work, among other writers, of nineteenth-century French poets like Baudelaire, Rimbaud and Laforgue. Or, going further back, to imagine how the poetry of Spenser, Shakespeare, Donne and Herbert, for example, might have been written without the pioneering work of the poets Wyatt and Surrey in discovering Italian Renaissance poetry. It matters, too, because such discoveries and influences do not only encourage mutual understanding, but also the recognition of what the former Chief Rabbi, Lord Sacks, has called 'the dignity of difference'.

The twentieth-century Spanish poet Federico García Lorca wished to acknowledge Spain's Arabic cultural heritage in his work and one of the ways he did so was to use the form of the *ghazal*. The greatest exponent of the *ghazal* in Persian poetry was Hafiz, a near contemporary of the English poet Geoffrey Chaucer, who lived under the rule of Timur Lenk, better known to English-language readers as Tamburlaine or Tamerlane. Hafiz's work is still read and admired in the Persian-speaking world today, where his *Divan* is regularly resorted to as a source of wisdom and advice. When Goethe read the *ghazals* of Hafiz in Joseph von Hammer's German translation in 1814, they were a revelation. Here was the German poet's 'twin', but also his guide and, alongside Marianne von Willemer, his inspiration.

A New Divan is a multilingual publication, consequently we did not need only to commission the original poems, but English-language poets to create new poems in English. Again, we did not want only to approach those who knew the languages concerned but to encourage a wide range of poets to engage with the project, and while some of them do translate directly into English, the majority have bravely undertaken this adventure with the help of fourteen expert translators, who generously agreed to provide annotated literal, or perhaps more accurately bridge translations. The twenty-four poems in English are, then, on a linguistic spectrum running from the two written originally in English, through direct translations, to poems written with some knowledge of the original language to poems created solely in response to the bridge translations and the shape and sound of the original poems. The English-language poets were given considerable freedom, but it is a mark of the quality of the original texts, as it is of the English poems themselves, that the poets have tended to stay close to the originals.

Finally, just as the first edition of Goethe's book contained 'Notes and Essays for a Better Understanding of the *West-Eastern Divan*', so *A New Divan* contains a number of essays. They provide valuable context and range from accounts of the original 'Western' response to Joseph von Hammer's translations of Hafiz and the 'Eastern' response to Goethe's *Divan*, to explorations of the challenges and opportunities presented by translating poetry from the 'East' into 'Western' languages and vice versa.

We hope that the book you now hold in your hands will give as much pleasure to read as it did to create.

Barbara Schwepcke and Bill Swainson, London, 18 March 2019

ACKNOWLEDGEMENTS

It would not have been possible to make *A New Divan* without the help of the wider community of poets, translators and editors. Our two general advisors were the Mexican-British poet Michael Schmidt, director of Carcanet Press, and the German poet Joachim Sartorius, formerly director of the Goethe Institut in Germany. The anthology has also benefited beyond measure from the detailed advice and constant encouragement of Margaret Obank and Samuel Shimon of *Banipal* magazine, Narguess Farzad of SOAS and Sasha Dugdale, former editor of *Modern Poetry in Translation*. Grateful thanks also go to Maureen Freely, Professor of Comparative Literature at Warwick University and President of English PEN, and to Erica Hesketh, Director of the Poetry Translation Centre. And as the project grew it was possible to call on the knowledge and expertise of the poets and translators themselves. To all of them the editors are extremely grateful.

The publishers acknowledge the editors of the publications in which some of the poems in this book first appeared:

Banipal: Reza Mohammadi / Nick Laird, 'Smoke' and Amjad
Nasser / Fady Joudah, 'Iron Horses'
New Statesman: Clara Janés / Lavinia Greenlaw, 'The Song of the
One Who Pours the Wine'
PN Review: Mohammed Bennis / Sinéad Morrissey, 'Aubade'
and Abbas Beydoun /Bill Manhire, 'Suleika and Marilyn',
Poetry Review: Khaled Mattawa, 'Easter Sunday, Rajab in
Mid-Moon'
Times Literary Supplement: Antonella Anedda / Jamie
McKendrick, from 'Three Ghazals'
Words Without Borders Daily: Gonca Özmen / Jo Shapcott,
'Knowingly, Willingly'

Acknowledgement is also made for permission to reproduce in the essay by Robyn Creswell extracts from 'The Stars above the Empty Quarter', "'Sii romantico, Seidel, tanto per cambiare'", and 'Mu'allaqa' from *Poems 1959–2009* by Frederick Seidel. Copyright © 2009 by Frederick Seidel. Reprinted by permission of Farrar, Straus and Giroux.

BIOGRAPHICAL NOTES

Alireza Abiz is an Iranian poet, literary critic and translator living in London. He studied English Literature in Mashhad and Tehran universities and received his PhD in Creative Writing (Poetry) from Newcastle University. He has published six collections of poetry in Persian, including *Black Line – London Underground* and *The Pomegranate of Bajestan*. He has translated a number of poets including Rainer Maria Rilke, Basil Bunting, Derek Walcott, Allen Ginsberg and C.K. Williams into Persian. He has written extensively on Persian contemporary literature and culture. His scholarly book, *Censorship of Literature in Post-Revolutionary Iran: Politics and Culture since 1979*, is forthcoming from I. B. Tauris.

Adonis was born Ali Ahmad Said Esber in Qassabin village, Syria, in 1930. He adopted the name Adonis when he was seventeen. He has been writing poetry for more than seventy-five years and is referred to as 'the grand old man of poetry, secularism and free speech in the Arab world'. He co-edited the influential *Sh'ir* poetry magazine and later established and edited the equally important *Mawaqif*. He is the author of many collections of poetry, and has published works of criticism, essays and translations. His work is translated into many languages, including in English *Adonis: Selected Poems, An Introduction to Arab Poetics, Sufism and Surrealism, Violence and Islam* and *Concerto Al-Quds*. He has received numerous awards, including France's Chevalier of the Légion d'Honneur (2012), Turkey's Nazim Hikmet Prize (1994), Germany's Goethe Prize (Frankfurt, 2011), the US PEN/Nabokov International Literature Lifetime Achievement Award (2017) and China's Poetry and People Award (2018).

Nujoom Alghanem is a poet, artist and film director from the UAE. She was born in Dubai in 1962, graduated from Ohio University in the USA with a BA in Video Production in 1996 and received an MA in Film Production, from Griffith University, Australia, in 1999. Although her career began in journalism, she now works as a film director and cultural consultant. An active and well-established writer and filmmaker in the Arab world, since 1989 she has published eight collections of poetry in Arabic, the most recent of which is called in English *I Fall Into Myself* (2012). An edition of her poems has appeared in Spanish, *Lo que queda del reproche* (Editorial Verbum, 2014), and a selection of poems has appeared in English in *Banipal* 42. She is on the board of the International Prize for Arabic Fiction (IPAF) and is a regular participant in the Emirates Airline Festival of Literature.

Fadhil al-Azzawi was born in Kirkuk in northern Iraq in 1940. He studied English literature at Baghdad University and cultural journalism at Leipzig University in Germany. He edited a number of magazines in Iraq and abroad and founded the literary magazine *Sh'ir 69* (Poetry 69). He was arrested many times and spent three years in prison for his political and cultural activities. He has published more than thirty books and many literary works of translation from German and English into Arabic. His poems and some of his books have been translated into many languages. Among his books in English are the poetry collection *Miracle Maker* (2003), translated by Khaled Mattawa, and three novels,

The Last of the Angels (2007), *Cell Block Five* (2008) and *The Traveller and the Innkeeper* (2011), all translated by William Maynard Hutchins. He left Iraq in 1977 and has lived in Berlin since 1983.

Khaled Aljbaili was born in Aleppo, Syria, in 1953. He studied at the Faculty of Humanities, University of Aleppo, Syria, and graduated with a BA in English Language and Literature. He obtained a Diploma in Translation at the same university. He was chief translator and interpreter at The International Center for Agricultural Research in the Dry Areas (ICARDA), Syria (1983–97). He then passed the United Nations international translators exam and worked as a translator/reviser at the UN's Arabic Translation Service in New York (1998–2015). He has translated more than sixty books (mainly literature and history), along with hundreds of articles, booklets and short stories from English into Arabic. Currently he works as a freelance translator and lives in California, USA.

Antonella Anedda (Anedda-Angioy) is the author of six volumes of poetry as well as numerous books of essays and translations from classical as well as modern poets. Born in Rome in 1955 to a Sardinian family, the island and the archipelago La Maddalena feature often in her work, some of which is written in Logudorese. She is a lecturer at the University of Lugano. *Salva con nome* received the 2012 Viareggio-Repaci Prize. Others among her books have won the Montale, Dedalus, Dessi, Naples and Pushkin prizes. In 2014 Bloodaxe Books published *Archipelago*, a selection of her work, translated into English by Jamie McKendrick. Her most recent book of poems is *Historiae*.

Homero Aridjis was born in Contepec, Michoacán, in 1940 to a Greek father and a Mexican mother. After nearly losing his life at age ten in a shotgun accident, Aridjis became an avid reader and began to write poetry. Many of his fifty books of poetry and prose have been translated into fifteen languages. Among the literary and environmental prizes he has received are the Xavier Villaurrutia and Diana-Novedades (Mexico), the Roger Caillois (France), the Grinzane-Cavour (Italy), the Orion Society's John Hay Award and two Guggenheim Fellowships. He has been a visiting professor at Indiana University, New York University, Columbia University and the University of California, Irvine. Formerly Mexico's ambassador to The Netherlands, Switzerland and UNESCO, he was president of PEN International (1997–2003). Aridjis is the founder and president of the Group of 100 – writers, artists and scientists devoted to protection of the environment. His most recent books in English translation are *The Child Poet*, *News of the Earth*, *Maria the Monarch* and *A Time of Angels*.

Mourid Barghouti was born in Deir Ghassana near Ramallah, Palestine, in 1944. He has published fourteen books of poetry and his *Collected Works* came out in Beirut in 1997 and in Cairo 2013. *A Small Sun*, his first poetry book in English translation, was published by The Aldeburgh Poetry Trust (2003), translated by Radwa Ashour and W.S. Merwin, and followed by *Midnight and Other Poems*, also translated by Radwa Ashour (Arc Publications, 2008). In 2000 he received the Palestine Award for Poetry and his memoir *I Saw Ramallah* (1997) won the Naguib Mahfouz Medal for Literature. It has since been published in several languages including English, translated by Ahdaf Soueif, with a foreword by Edward Said

(American University in Cairo Press, Random House, New York, and Bloomsbury, London). It was followed by *I Was Born There, I Was Born Here*, translated by Humphrey Davies, with a foreword by John Berger (Bloomsbury, 2012).

Mohammed Bennis was born in Fez, Morocco, in 1948, and taught in the Faculty of Arts at Mohammed V University in Rabat (1980–2016). He is the author of forty books, among them fourteen poetry collections, some of which have been translated into French, German, Italian and Turkish, among other languages. He has also translated works from French, including the first translation into Arabic of *A Throw of the Dice* by Stéphane Mallarmé (Ypsilon Éditeur, Paris, 2007). In 1974 he founded the review *The New Culture*, and in 1985, together with other university professors and writers, he established the publishing house Dar Toubkal. In 1999, he was instrumental in the establishment UNESCO's World Poetry Day (21 March). Among awards he has received are El Primeo Feronia (Italy, 2007), the Al Owais Award (Dubai, 2008) and the Prix Max Jacob 'Étranger' (France, 2014). His most recent poetry collections are *Seven Birds* and *This Blue*.

Tara Bergin was born (1974) and grew up in Co. Dublin, Ireland. The process and influence of literary translation was the topic of her PhD research, and has preoccupied much of her writing since. She is the author of two poetry collections published by Carcanet Press, *This Is Yarrow* (2013) and *The Tragic Death of Eleanor Marx* (2017), which was shortlisted for the T.S. Eliot and Forward Prizes, and chosen as a Best Poetry Book of the year by *The Times* and the *Irish Times*. She lives in the Yorkshire Dales and lectures part-time at Newcastle University.

Abbas Beydoun was born in the village of Sur near Tyre in southern Lebanon in 1945. He studied Arabic Literature at the Lebanese University in Beirut, later receiving a Masters in Literature at the Sorbonne in Paris. He was involved in left-wing politics and was imprisoned for a time as a young man. A poet, novelist and journalist, he has published numerous volumes of poetry, some of which have been translated into a number of European languages, including a Selected Poems in Italian, a volume in German, several books including his epic work *Tyre* in French, and a volume of essays. English translations of his poetry have appeared in several issues of *Banipal* magazine and his novel *Tahlil damm* (2002) was translated by Max Weiss and published under the title *Blood Test* (Syracuse University Press, 2008), winning the Arkansas Arabic Translation Award. He has been cultural editor of the Beiruti newspaper *As-Safir* since 1997.

Charlotte Collins studied English Literature at Cambridge University and worked as a radio journalist in Germany and the UK before becoming a literary translator. She was awarded the 2017 Helen & Kurt Wolff Translator's Prize for *A Whole Life* by Robert Seethaler (Picador), which was also shortlisted for the Man Booker International and the International Dublin Literary Award. Her other translations include *The Tobacconist*, also by Seethaler, *Homeland* by Walter Kempowski, *The End of Loneliness* by Benedict Wells and Stefan Weidner's narrative essay *In the Greece of the East: A Journey through Jewish Ukraine*.

Robyn Creswell graduated from Brown University in 1999 and received a PhD in Comparative Literature from New York University in 2011. He is Assistant Professor of Comparative Literature at Yale University and the author of *City of Beginnings: Poetic Modernism in Beirut*. He is the translator of Abdelfattah Kilito's *The Clash of Images* and *The Tongue of Adam*, both from the French, as well as Sonallah Ibrahim's *That Smell and Notes from Prison*, from the Arabic. All three translations were published by New Directions. His essays and reviews have been published in the *New Yorker*, the *New York Review of Books* and the *New York Times Book Review*. He is a former fellow of the Cullman Center at the New York Public Library, and of the American Academy in Berlin, and a former poetry editor at the *Paris Review*.

Dick Davis was born in Portsmouth, England, in 1945. He read English Literature at Cambridge and subsequently spent eight years in Iran, where he met and married Afkham Darbandi, with whom he translated Attar's *The Conference of Birds*, before completing a PhD in Medieval Persian Literature at Manchester. He taught at a number of universities in the UK and the USA, retiring from Ohio State University in 2012 as Professor of Persian and Chair of the Department of Near Eastern Languages and Cultures. His award-winning translations from Persian include *Vis and Ramin, Faces of Love: Hafez and the Poets of Shiraz*, among others. He has published seven collections of his own poetry, all with Anvil, including *Seeing the World* (1980), which won the Royal Society of Literature's Heinemann Award for Poetry, and *A Trick of Sunlight: Poems 2001–2005*. His translations of poems by Fatameh Shams, *When They Broke Down the Door*, appeared in 2015.

Sasha Dugdale was born in Sussex in 1974. She is a poet, translator and editor and has published four collections of poetry, the most recent of which is *Joy* (Carcanet, 2017). *Joy* was a PBS Winter Choice and the collection is named after her long poem 'Joy' which won the Forward Prize for Best Single Poem in 2016. She translates poetry and plays from Russian and has worked with theatres across the UK and US on new productions of contemporary Russian drama. Her poetry translations were shortlisted for the Rossica and Popescu Prizes. She is currently working on translations of Maria Stepanova's poems for publication by Bloodaxe in 2019. She is a former editor of *Modern Poetry in Translation* and co-editor of the international anthology *Centres of Cataclysm* (Bloodaxe, 2016).

Paul Farley was born in Liverpool and studied at the Chelsea School of Art. He is the author of four collections of his poetry including *The Boy from the Chemist Is Here to See You* (1998) and *Dark Film* (2012), and a *Selected Poems* (2014), all published by Picador. His work has received many accolades, including the E.M. Forster Award from the American Academy of Arts & Letters and the 2009 Jerwood Prize for *Edgelands: Journeys into England's True Wilderness* (2011), co-authored with Michael Symmons Roberts. A regular broadcaster, he has written and hosted many arts features and documentaries for BBC Radio, and in 2012 presented a two-part programme called *Goethe and the West-Eastern Divan* for BBC Radio 3 (https://www.bbc.co.uk/programmes/601lodrs). He teaches at Lancaster University, where he is Professor of Poetry.

Narguess Farzad was born in Tehran, Iran, in 1960 and graduated with a degree in Persian Studies from SOAS, University of London. After an early career at the Persian Section of the BBC World Service, and then as a civil servant, she returned to SOAS, where, as the Senior Fellow in Persian, she teaches Persian language and poetry. Her publications include *Grammar of Modern Persian* (Hodder), 'Qeysar Aminpur and the Persian Poetry of Sacred Defence' (*British Journal of Middle Eastern Studies*), *Poems of Farzaneh Khojandi* (Enitharmon), introductory chapters for the series *Rumi's Little Book of Life: The Garden of the Soul, the Heart and the Spirit; A Little Book of Mystical Secrets: Rumi, Shams of Tabriz, and the Path of Ecstasy* and *Little Book of Rumi, Stories of the Masnavi* (Red Wheel Weiser). She regularly contributes to cultural programmes on BBC Radio 3 and Radio 4 and is on the editorial board of the *Middle East in London*.

Elaine Feinstein was born in 1930 in Liverpool. She was educated at Wyggeston Grammar School for Girls, Leicester, and won an Exhibition to Newnham College, Cambridge, in 1949. She began publishing in the 1950. Since then, she has travelled to major festivals across the globe. Her fifteenth book of poems was *The Clinic, Memory* (Carcanet, 2017). Her award-winning versions of Marina Tsvetaeva's poems (OUP, 1970) was a *New York Times* Book of the Year and remains in print. She has written fifteen novels, many plays for radio and TV and five biographies, including *Ted Hughes: The Life of a Poet* and *Anna of all the Russias: A life of Anna Akhmatova* (both Weidenfeld). She is a Fellow of the Royal Society of Literature and was a member of its Council.

Maureen Freely is a writer with seven novels to her name and many other strings to her bow. Well known as a translator of the Turkish Nobel Laureate Orhan Pamuk, she has also brought into English several classics and works by Turkey's rising stars. For many years she worked as a journalist in London, writing about literature, social justice and human rights. As chair of the Translator's Association and more recently as President and Chair of English PEN, she has campaigned for writers and freedom of expression internationally. She teaches at the University of Warwick.

Angélica Freitas was born in Pelotas, Brazil, in 1973. She studied Journalism at Universidade Federal do Rio Grande do Sul and worked for several years as a reporter in Porto Alegre and then São Paulo. She left Brazil in 2006, living temporarily in the Netherlands, Bolivia and Argentina, before returning to Pelotas, where she now lives. She is the author of two poetry collections, *um útero é do tamanho de um punho* (An Uterus Is the Size of a Fist) and *Rilke Shake*, which was translated into English by Hilary Kaplan, and won the 2016 Best Translated Book Award, granted by the University of Rochester, USA. She is also the author of a graphic novel, *Guadalupe*, and coedits the poetry journal *Modo de Usar & Co*. Her poems have been translated into French, German, Romanian and Spanish, and in English have appeared in *Modern Poetry in Translation*, *Granta* and *Poetry*, among other publications.

Daisy Fried is the author of three books of poetry: *She Didn't Mean to Do It*, which won the 1999 Agnes Lynch Starrett Prize, *My Brother is Getting Arrested Again*, a finalist for the 2006 National Book Critics Circle Award, and *Women's Poetry: Poems and Advice*, named by *Library Journal* as one of the five best poetry books of 2013. She has been awarded Guggenheim, Hodder and Pew Fellowships, a Pushcart Prize, the Cohen Award from *Ploughshares*, and the Editors Prize for a feature article from *Poetry*, for 'Sing, God-Awful Muse', about reading *Paradise Lost*, breast-feeding and the importance of difficulty. She is poetry editor for the literary resistance journal *Scoundrel Time*, and occasionally reviews poetry for the *New York Times*, *Poetry* and elsewhere. A member of the faculty of the Warren Wilson College MFA Program for Writers, she lives in Philadelphia.

Iain Galbraith was born in Glasgow in 1956 and grew up in Arrochar on the west coast of Scotland. He now lives in Wiesbaden, Germany. His poems have appeared in *Poetry Review*, the *Times Literary Supplement*, *Edinburgh Review* and *PN Review*. After decades of publishing in magazines and anthologies, his first volume of poetry, *The True Height of the Ear* (Arc) appeared in 2018. Among his book-length translations are Alfred Kolleritsch's *Selected Poems* (Shearsman), W. G. Sebald's *Across the Land and the Water. Selected Poems 1964–2001* (Hamish Hamilton), Jan Wagner's *Self-portrait with a Swarm of Bees* (Arc) and, most recently, Esther Kinsky's novel *River* (Fitzcarraldo). He has received several prizes and awards, including the Stephen Spender Prize (2014), the Popescu Prize for European Poetry Translation (2015), the Schlegel-Tieck Prize (2016) and a PEN/Heim Translation Fund Grant (2017).

Rajmohan Gandhi was born in New Delhi in 1935. A historian and biographer, he divides his time between India and the United States, where he is a professor at the University of Illinois at Urbana-Champaign. He first wrote on Muhammad Iqbal in *Eight Lives: A Study of the Hindu-Muslim Encounter* (1986). Other books by him include *Gandhi: The Man, his People and the Empire* (2007), *Punjab: A History from Aurangzeb to Mountbatten* (2013), *Patel: A Life* (1990) and *Understanding the Founding Fathers: An Enquiry into the Indian Republic's Beginnings* (2016). In the 1990s he served as a member of the Rajya Sabha, the upper house of the Indian parliament.

Reem Ghanayem was born in Palestine in 1982. She is a poet, translator and researcher in the fields of Arabic and English Literature. Her PhD thesis concentrated on the theatre of the absurd and its different ways of representation. She has published two poetry collections: *Mag – a Life of Exiles* and *Prophecies: Self Portraits*. Her translations from English into Arabic include James Joyce's *Chamber Music+Pomes Pennyeach*, an anthology of African American Poetry, and Richard Wright's *This Other World*, as well as fiction by Charles Bukowski and William Burroughs, and Richard Wright's Haiku book *This Other World*. She works as chief editor in the short story project website (https://www.shortstoryproject.com/).

Jorie Graham was born in New York in 1950. She has published fourteen collections of poetry including *The Dream of the Unified Field* which was awarded the 1996 Pulitzer Prize. Most recently she published *From the New World: Selected Poems 1976–2014* and *FAST*. Her work is widely translated and she teaches at Harvard University, where she is Boylston professor in the Department of English and American Literature and Language. She lives in Massachusetts.

Lavinia Greenlaw was born in London in 1962. She has an MA in seventeenth-century art from the Courtauld Institute, and was the first artist-in-residence at the Science Museum. Her interest in vision, scientific process and image-making led to fellowships from Wellcome and NESTA. Her immersive soundwork *Audio Obscura*, received the 2011 Ted Hughes Award. Her poetry includes *The Casual Perfect* and *A Double Sorrow: Troilus and Criseyde*. Her most recent collection, *The Built Moment*, was published by Faber in February 2019. Her other works include *Questions of Travel: William Morris in Iceland, The Importance of Music to Girls* and the novel *In the City of Love's Sleep* (2018). She has written for the *London Review of Books,* the *New Yorker* and *Frieze* among other publications.

Durs Grünbein was born in Dresden in 1962 and lives in Berlin and Rome. After the decline of the Soviet Empire he travelled in Europe, South Asia and the United States. Since 2005 he has been Professor of Poetics and Aesthetics at the Kunstakademie Düsseldorf. Since 2009 he has been a member of the Pour le Mérite Order for Science and Arts in Germany. He has published fifteen collections of poetry, a diary, a memoir and four books of essays. He has also translated works by John Ashbery, Samuel Beckett, Henri Michaux and Wallace Stevens, and classic texts by Aeschylus, Juvenal and Seneca. He has received many literary prizes, including the 1995 Georg Büchner Prize, the 2004 Nietzsche Prize, the 2005 Hölderlin Prize, Italy's 2006 Pier Paolo Pasolini Prize and Sweden's 2012 Tranströmer Prize. His poetry has been translated into English by Michael Hofmann (*Ashes for Breakfast*, Faber) and Michael Eskin (*Mortal Diamond*, Upper Westside Philosophers, Inc.), and also into many other languages.

Kadhim J. Hassan is a poet, literary critic and translator. Born in southern Iraq in 1955, he has lived in France for more than forty years. A professor of classical Arabic literature and literary translation in Paris at the Institut National des Langues et Civilisations Orientales (INALCO), he has translated Dante, Rimbaud and Rilke, among others, into Arabic. He has written several essays on the poetics of translation, among them *La Part de l'étranger – la traduction de la poésie dans la culture arabe* (Editions Actes Sud/Sindbad, 2007). In 2016, he was awarded the Gerardo de Cremona international prize for translation.

Brian Henry is the author of ten books of poetry, most recently *Static & Snow* (Black Ocean, 2015). He co-edited the international magazine *Verse* (1995–2017) and established the Tomaž Šalamun Prize in 2015. His translation of Aleš Šteger's *The Book of Things* (BOA Editions, 2010) won that year's Best Translated Book Award. He also has translated Tomaž Šalamun's *Woods and Chalices* (Harcourt, 2008) and Aleš Debeljak's *Smugglers* (BOA, 2015). His poetry and translations have received numerous honours, including a National Endowment for the Arts fellowship, a Howard Foundation grant, the Alice Fay di Castagnola Award, the Cecil B. Hemley Memorial Award, the Carole Weinstein Poetry Prize, the George Bogin Memorial Award and a Slovenian Academy of Arts and Sciences grant.

Kathleen Jamie, poet and essayist, was born in the west of Scotland in 1962. Her poetry collections to date include *The Tree House* (2004), which won the Forward prize, and *The Overhaul* (2012), which won the Costa Poetry Prize. Her non-fiction includes the highly acclaimed books *Findings* and *Sightlines*, both regarded as important contributions to the 'new nature writing'. Her most recent poetry collection, *The Bonniest Companie* appeared in 2015, and won the Saltire Scottish Book of the Year Award.

Clara Janés was born in Barcelona in 1940 and has published some forty volumes of poetry, several collections of essays and three novels. Among awards she has received are the Gold Medal of Merit in Fine Arts (2004), the Teresa de Ávila National Literary Prize (2007) and the Francisco Pino Prize for Experimental Poetry (2011). In 2014 she was enrolled as a Member of Honour by the International Centre for Transdisciplinary Research (CIRET) in Paris, and since 2015 she has been a member of the Spanish Royal Academy. She is also well known as translator of poetry, especially from Czech but also from French, English, Portuguese, Italian and, with other specialists, from Turkish and Iranian (both contemporary and ancient mystical poets). She has been awarded the Turkish Tutav Foundation Prize (1992), Spain's National Translation Prize (1997), the First Category Medal of Merit from the Czech Republic (2000) and also the Sapere Aude prize (2017).

Fady Joudah is a Palestinian American and a practising physician who lives with his wife and children in Houston, TX. He has published four collections of original poetry and five volumes in translation from the Arabic. For his poetry and translation he has received the Yale Series prize, a Guggenheim Fellowship, the Griffin Poetry prize, the Saif Ghobash Banipal Prize for Arabic Literary Translation award and a PEN USA award among others. His current collection is *Footnotes in the Order of Disappearance* (Milkweed Editions, 2018).

Hilary Kaplan was born in Los Angeles, California. She is the translator of *The Territory Is Not the Map* by Marília Garcia and *Rilke Shake* by Angélica Freitas, which won the National Translation Award and the Best Translated Book Award in 2016. Her most recent translation is *46750*, a collaboration between photographer João Pina and poet Viviane Salles. She has contributed to *Granta*, *Modern Poetry in Translation* and BBC Radio 4. Her other translations of Brazilian prose and poetry include Paloma Vidal's short story collection, *Ghosts*, and poems by Ricardo Domeneck and Claudia Roquette-Pinto. She studied Comparative Literature at Yale and Brown, and Creative Writing: Poetry at San Francisco State University. She received a PEN Translation Fund award and a Rumos Literatura fellowship in literary criticism from Itaú Cultural.

Jaan Kaplinski was born in 1941 in Tartu to an Estonian mother and a Polish father who disappeared in the Gulag Archipelago during the Second World War. He studied linguistics at Tartu University and worked as a researcher in linguistics, and as a sociologist, ecologist and translator from several languages into Estonian. During *perestroika* and the Estonian national revival he was active as a journalist both at home and abroad, and then a deputy of the Estonian Parliament (1992–5). He has lectured on the history of Western civilisation at Tartu University and published several books of poetry and essays in Estonian, Russian, Finnish and English. His work has been translated into English, Norwegian, Swedish, Latvian, Russian, Czech, Japanese, Hebrew and other languages. He has travelled in many countries, including China, Turkey, New Zealand, Peru and parts of Russia and has been awarded several literary prizes at home and abroad, among others the Vilenica prize (Slovenia), the Max Jacob prize (France) and the Russian Prize (for his book of poetry written in Russian).

Nick Laird was born in County Tyrone, Northern Ireland, in 1975. He is a poet, novelist, screenwriter and former lawyer. His novels are *Utterly Monkey, Glover's Mistake* and *Modern Gods*, and his poetry collections are *To a Fault, On Purpose, Go Giants* and *Feel Free*. He co-edited the anthology, *The Zoo of the New* with Don Paterson. Awards for his writing include the Betty Trask Prize, the Rooney Prize for Irish Literature, the Geoffrey Faber Memorial Prize, the Somerset Maugham award, the Ireland Chair of Poetry Prize and a Guggenheim fellowship. His poem-film, *Troubles: The Life After*, a collaboration with Brian Hill, was shown on BBC2 in October 2018. He is Writer-in-Residence at New York University and Professor of Creative Writing at the Seamus Heaney Centre at Queens University, Belfast.

Karen Leeder is a writer, translator and academic. Born in 1962, she teaches German at New College, Oxford where she works especially on modern poetry and leads the project 'Mediating Modern Poetry' (mmp.mml.ox.ac.uk). She translates contemporary German literature into English, including works by Volker Braun, Michael Krüger and Raoul Schrott. Her most recent translations include Evelyn Schlag's *All Under one Roof* (Carcanet) which was the PBS summer translation selection (2018) and she was given an English PEN award and an American PEN/Heim award for her translations from Ulrike Almut Sandig's *Dickicht / Thick of it* (Seagull, 2018). Her translations of Durs Grünbein stretch back over a decade and were awarded the Stephen Spender Prize (2011) and the John Frederik Nims Memorial Prize (2018).

Bill Manhire was born in Invercargill, New Zealand, in 1946. He was educated at the University of Otago (English literature) and University College London (Old Norse studies), and taught for many years at Victoria University of Wellington, where he led the International Institute of Modern Letters, which is home to the university's well-known creative writing programme. He was New Zealand's inaugural poet laureate, and in that capacity briefly visited the South Pole. He has published many books of poetry and short fiction, most recently *Some Things to Place in a Coffin* and *The Stories of Bill Manhire*. He has also edited a number of anthologies, including *The Wide White Page: Writers Imagine Antarctica*.

Catherine Mansfield is a translator, copyeditor and communications professional. Her translations include *China's Silent Army* by Juan Pablo Cardenal and Heriberto Araújo (Penguin Press, 2013) and *A History of the World for Rebels and Somnambulists* by Jesús del Campo (Telegram, 2008). She has also translated short works of fiction and non-fiction by authors including Brenda Lozano, Rafael Pérez Gay and Juan Pablo Anaya for *Words Without Borders* and *Mexico 20* (Pushkin 2015). She is co-founder of a creative translation agency called ZigZag Translations, which she set up while living in Bogotá, Colombia; she now lives in London.

Khaled Mattawa was born in Benghazi, Libya, in 1964 and emigrated to the US in 1979, where he studied at the University of Tennessee at Chattanooga, taking a Masters in English and an MFA in creative writing at Indiana University. He received a PhD from Duke University and currently teaches in the graduate creative writing program at the University of Michigan. He is the author of four books of poetry, the latest of which, *Tocqueville*, won the 2010 San Francisco Poetry Center Prize. Mattawa has translated eleven volumes of contemporary Arabic poetry, including Adonis's *Selected Poems* and *Concerto Al-Quds*, Iman Mersal's *These Are Not Oranges My Love* and Fadhil al-Azzawi's *Miracle Maker*. His book *Mahmoud Darwish: The Poet's Arts and His Nation* was a finalist for the Pegasus Prize. A MacArthur fellow, his other awards include the Academy of American Poets Fellowship prize and the PEN Award for Poetry in Translation.

Jamie McKendrick was born in Liverpool in 1955 and has published seven books of poetry including *The Marble Fly*, which won the 1997 Forward Prize, *Out There* which won the 2012 Hawthornden Prize and most recently *Anomaly* (2018), the latter two published by Faber. He edited *The Faber Book of 20th-Century Italian Poems* in 2004, and his translation of Giorgio Bassani's *The Novel of Ferrara* was published this year. His translation of Valerio Magrelli's poems, *The Embrace* (Faber, 2009) won the Oxford-Weidenfeld Prize and the John Florio Prize, and his translation of Antonella Anedda's poems, *Archipelago* (Bloodaxe, 2014), also won the John Florio Prize.

Anne McLean was born in Toronto, Canada, in 1962. She has translated Latin American and Spanish novels, stories, memoirs and other writings by many authors including Héctor Abad, Javier Cercas, Julio Cortázar, Gabriel García Márquez, Juan Gabriel Vásquez and Enrique Vila-Matas. She has twice won the *Independent* Foreign Fiction Prize, for *Soldiers of Salamis* by Javier Cercas (2004) and for *The Armies* by Evelio Rosero (2009) and twice won the Valle Inclán Prize, for *Soldiers of Salamis* and *Outlaws* (2015), both by Javier Cercas. In 2014 she shared the International Dublin IMPAC Literary Award with Juan Gabriel Vásquez for her translation of his novel *The Sound of Things Falling*. She was awarded the Spanish Cross of the Order of Civil Merit in 2012.

Iman Mersal was born in Egypt in 1966. She is a poet, essayist, translator and literary scholar, and Professor of Arabic Language and Literature at the University of Alberta, Canada. She is the author of five books of poetry in Arabic, selections from which have been translated into several languages, including Spanish, French, Hebrew and Hindi. In English translation, her poems have appeared in *Parnassus, Paris Review, The Nation, American Poetry Review* and *The Kenyon Review*. A selection of Mersal's poetry, entitled *These Are Not Oranges, My Love*, translated by the poet Khaled Mattawa, was published in 2008 (Sheep Meadow Press). Her most recent publications include an Arabic translation of Charles Simic's memoir, *A Fly in the Soup* (Al Kotob Khan, 2016), and a group of essays, *How to mend: on motherhood and its ghosts* (Kayfa Ta and Mophradat, 2017).

Reza Mohammadi was born in Kandahar, Afghanistan, in 1979. He studied Islamic Law and then Philosophy in Iran before obtaining an MA in Globalisation from London Metropolitan University. Regarded as one of the most exciting younger poets writing in Persian, his three collections of poetry have gained him many awards, including Iran's prize for the best young poet in 1996 and 1997, an award from the Afghan Ministry of Culture in 2004 and national medals from the last two Presidents of Afghanistan. Today he is President of the Afghanistan Writers Union. In 2012 a selection of his work, translated into English by Nick Laird with Hamid Kabir, appeared as a Poetry Translation Centre Chapbook, *Poems: Reza Mohammadi*. He is also a prolific journalist and cultural commentator, whose articles have appeared in journals in Afghanistan and Iran, and in English in the *Guardian*.

Sinéad Morrissey was born in Northern Ireland in 1972 and educated at Trinity College, Dublin. She has published six collections of poetry, all with Carcanet: *There Was Fire in Vancouver* (1996); *Between Here and There* (2002); *The State of the Prisons* (2005); *Through the Square Window* (2009); *Parallax* (2013) and *On Balance* (2017). Her awards include the *Irish Times* Poetry Now Award (2009, 2013) and the T.S. Eliot Prize (2013). In 2016 she received the E.M. Forster Award from the American Academy of Arts and Letters. *On Balance* was awarded the Forward Prize in 2017. She has served as Belfast Poet Laureate (2013–14) and is currently Director of the Newcastle Centre for the Literary Arts at Newcastle University.

Hafez Mousavi was born in 1955 in the northern city of Roudbar in Iran. He studied Persian Language and Literature at Shahid Beheshti University in Tehran. He has published eight books of poetry, three books in the field of literary research and criticism and one book of fiction for children. In addition to numerous literary and critical essays and articles written for various journals in Iran, he co-founded the contemporary poetry magazine *Ahang-e Digar* with Shams Langeroodi and Shahab Mogharabin, founded *Vazna*, Iran's first online poetry journal, and for four years was editor-in-chief of the important Iranian literary journal, *Karnameh* (1998–2004). He is a member of the Iranian Writers Association and teaches a poetry workshop at the independent Karnameh Institute of Arts & Culture in Tehran. English translations of his poem can be found in *The Poetry of Hafez Moosavi: Middle East Poems and other Poems* (CreateSpace Independent Publishing Platform, 2013).

Suneela Mubayi studied Arabic literature at the Department of Middle Eastern and Islamic Studies at New York University, where she recently received a PhD, completing a thesis on the intersection of classical and modern Arabic poetry. She has translated poems and short stories between Arabic, English and Urdu, which have been published in *Banipal*, *Beirut39*, *Jadaliyya*, *Rusted Radishes* and elsewhere. She wishes to re-establish the position of Arabic as a vehicular language of the global South, the role it played for many centuries.

Doireann Ní Ghríofa is a bilingual Irish writer, born in Galway, Ireland, in 1981. She writes both prose and poetry, in both Irish and English, and her books explore birth, death, desire and domesticity. Among her awards are the Rooney Prize for Irish Literature, a Seamus Heaney Fellowship, and the Ostana Prize (Italy). Her latest books are *Lies* (Dedalus Press), which draws on a decade of her Irish language poems in translation, and 9 *Silences* (Salvage Press), a collaborative book with acclaimed visual artist Alice Maher. Her artistic practice often involves cross-disciplinary collaborations, fusing poetry with film, dance, music and visual art, and she has been invited to perform her work internationally, most recently in Scotland, Paris, Italy and New Zealand. She lives in Cork with her husband and four young children.

Lulu Norman is a translator, writer and editor, with a particular interest in North African and Middle Eastern literature. After studying at UCL and gaining her diploma in translation, she translated books by Albert Cossery, Amin Maalouf and Tahar Ben Jelloun, and also the songs of Serge Gainsbourg. She has written reviews and feature articles on literature and travel for the *LRB, Independent, Guardian* and *Banipal*, amongst others, and has edited titles for Saqi and Penguin Classics. Her translation of Mahi Binebine's *Welcome to Paradise* (Granta) was shortlisted for the *Independent* Foreign Fiction Prize in 2003 and in 2013 her translation of Binebine's *Horses of God* received an English PEN Award, was runner-up for the Scott Montcrieff and was shortlisted for the Best Translated Book Award and featured in World Literature Today's 75 Notable Translations. She lives in London.

Amjad Nasser was born in Al-Turra, Jordan, in 1955 and has worked as a journalist in Beirut and Cyprus. A major force in contemporary Arab writing, he has published eight collections of poetry, two books of travel writing and two novels. Two collections of his poetry have appeared in English, *Shepherd of Solitude: Selected Poems* (Banipal, 2009), translated by Khaled Mattawa, and *A Map of Signs and Scents* (Northwestern, 2016), translated by Fady Joudah and Khaled Mattawa. His novel, first published in Arabic in 2011, appeared in English, translated by Jonathan Wright, as *Land of No Rain* (Bloomsbury Qatar Foundation Publishing, 2014). In the same year, he was invited to inaugurate New York University's Gallatin Global Writers series but was denied entry to the United States by the Department of Homeland Security amid vociferous protest from PEN America Center and other organisations.

Gilles Ortlieb was born in Morocco in 1953. He studied Classics at the Sorbonne, and after a period in which he was variously employed, interspersed by trips to Greece and the Mediterranean, he spent many years in Luxembourg where he worked as a translator for the European Union. He has published some twenty books in a wide range of genres, including poems, stories, essays and notebooks; these include *Soldats et autres récits, Et tout le tremblement* (Le Bruit du Temps, 2014 and 2016), *Place au cirque, Au Grand Miroir, Tombeau des anges* (Gallimard, 2002, 2005 and 2011) and *Sous le crible, Le Train des jours, Ângelo* (Finitude, 2008, 2010, 2018). He has made a number of translations into French, including, from the Greek, works by Constantin Cavafy, George Seferis and Thanassis Valtinos, and from the English, by Patrick McGuinness and Stephen Romer.

Gonca Özmen was born in Burdur, Turkey, in 1982. She studied English Language and Literature at Istanbul University, receiving an MA in 2008 and a PhD in 2016. Her first poem was published in 1997 and in 1999 she received the Ali Rıza Ertan Poetry Prize. Her first collection *Kuytumda* (In My Nook, 2000) won the Orhan Murat Arıburnu Poetry Prize and in 2003 she received Istanbul University's Berna Moran Poetry Prize. Her second collection *Belki Sessiz* (Maybe Silent) appeared in 2008 and was published in German, translated by Monika Carbe, in 2017. A selection of her poems in English, *The Sea Within* (Shearsman), translated by George Messo, appeared in 2011. She is a member of the advisory board of Bursa Nilüfer International Poetry Festival and the magazine, *Turkish Poetry Today*. She is also a member of the Three Seas Writers' and Translators' Council in Rhodes, Greece.

Don Paterson was born in Dundee in 1963. His poetry collections include *Landing Light*, *Rain* and *40 Sonnets*, as well as versions of Machado (*The Eyes*) and Rilke (*Orpheus*); he is also the author of several books of aphorism, the most recently *The Fall at Home*; his critical writing includes *Reading Shakespeare's Sonnets* and *The Poem: Lyric, Sign, Metre*. His poetry has been the recipient of several awards, including the T.S. Eliot Prize on two occasions. He is Professor of Poetry at the University of St Andrews, poetry editor at Picador Macmillan, and has for many years also worked as a jazz musician and composer.

Robin Robertson, born in 1955, is from the north-east coast of Scotland. A Fellow of the Royal Society of Literature, he has published six books of poetry with Picador and received a number of accolades, including the Petrarca-Preis, the E.M. Forster Award from the American Academy of Arts and Letters, and all three Forward Prizes. He has also edited a collection of essays, *Mortification: Writers' Stories of Their Public Shame*, translated two plays of Euripides, *Medea* and the *Bacchae*, and, in 2006, published *The Deleted World*, a selection of free English versions of poems by the Nobel laureate Tomas Tranströmer. His selected poems, *Sailing the Forest*, came out in 2014. In 2018 *The Long Take* won the Roehampton Poetry Prize and was shortlisted for the Man Booker Prize and the Goldsmiths Prize.

Raoul Schrott was born 1964 in Austria, grew up in Tunisia, studied in Norwich and Paris, was secretary of Philippe Soupault, gained a PhD, teaches Comparative Literature in Tübingen, Bern and Innsbruck and has received most of the major German literary awards. He is the author of many collections of poetry, including *Hotels*, *Tropen*, *Weissbuch* and *Die Kunst an nichts zu glauben* (a selection from these is forthcoming from Seagull Books); novels, including *Finis Terrae*, *Tristan da Cunha*, *Die Wüste Lop Nor* (published in English as *The Desert of Lop* by Picador); and essays. His translations include, *Gilgamesh*, *The Iliad*, *Theogony* and Derek Walcott's *Midsummer*. His latest work is *Erste Erde. Epos* (forthcoming in English translation as *First Earth. Epic* from Seagull), narrates through different characters and voices what we know about our origins, from the Big Bang to the formation of the sun and the earth, the evolution of life up to cave paintings and the invention of writing.

Fatemeh Shams was born in Mashhad (Khorasan), Iran, in 1983. She won the silver medal in the national Olympiad of Persian literature at the age of seventeen. She completed her BA in sociology at Tehran University and migrated to the UK in 2006 to pursue higher education. In 2007, she received the Arabic language award from Bourguiba School, Tunisia, where she completed advanced level Arabic. She gained a DPhil in the field of Oriental Studies at the University of Oxford in 2015 and is currently assistant professor of modern Persian literature at the University of Pennsylvania. She is the author of three collections of poetry, including *When They Broke Down the Door* (translated into English by Dick Davis), which received the Latifeh Yarshater Book Award in 2016. She also received the Jaleh Esfahani poetry prize in 2012. Her work has so far been translated into English, Arabic and Kurdish.

Jo Shapcott was born in London in 1953 and educated at Trinity College, Dublin, and St Hilda's College, Oxford, and later won a Harkness Fellowship to Harvard University. Poems from her three award-winning collections, *Electroplating the Baby* (1988), *Phrase Book* (1992) and *My Life Asleep* (1998) are gathered in a selected poems, *Her Book* (2000). She has won a number of literary prizes including the Commonwealth Writers' Prize for Best First Collection, the Forward Prize for Best Collection and the National Poetry Competition (twice). *Tender Taxes*, her versions of Rilke, was published in 2001. Her most recent collection, *Of Mutability*, was published by Faber in 2010 and won the Costa Book Award. In 2011 she was awarded the Queen's Gold Medal for Poetry.

Aleš Šteger was born in Pluj, Slovenia, in 1973. A poet and prose writer, he is now based in Ljubljana. His work has been widely translated and appeared in the *New Yorker, Boston Review, Süddeutsche Zeitung* and many other publications. In 2016 he was awarded the International Bienek Prize for poetry by the Bavarian Academy of Arts. Among other prizes the English translation by Brian Henry of his poetry collection *Knjiga reči, The Book of Things* (BOA Editions, 2010), won two leading US translation awards (BTBA and AATSEL). Three of his sixteen other books have been published in English tramslation: *Berlin* (stories), *Essential Baggage* (poetry) and *Absolution* (novel). He works in various artforms, including a large-scale installation at the International Kochi-Muziris Arts Biennale in India, and collaborations with musicians (Godalika, Uroš Rojko, Peter N. Gruber) and the film director Peter Zach. He is the initiator of the European platform for poetry Versopolis.

Matthew Sweeney (1952–2018) was born in Co. Donegal, Ireland. He read English and German at the Polytechnic of North London, studying for a year at the University of Freiburg, Germany. He was the author of many collections of poetry, including *Cacti, The Bridal Suite* and *Black Moon* which was shortlisted for the T.S. Eliot Prize. He also wrote poetry and novels for children, including *The Flying Spring Onion, The Snow Vulture* and *Fox*. He compiled two anthologies for Faber, *Emergency Kit: Poems for Strange Times* (with Jo Shapcott) and *The New Faber Book of Children's Verse*. His last two books, published shortly before he died, were *My Life as an Artist* and *King of a Rainy Country*.

Mbarek Sryfi, holds a PhD in Arabic literature from the University of Pennsylvania, where he is currently a lecturer in Foreign Languages. His translations have appeared in *CELAAN, Metamorphoses*, meadmagazine.org, *World Literature Today* and *Banipal*. He has published with Roger Allen *Monarch of the Square: An Anthology of Muhammad Zafzaf's Short Stories* (Syracuse University Press, 2014) and Zafzaf's *The Elusive Fox* (Syracuse University Press, 2016). And with Eric Sellin, Abdelfattah Kilito's *Arabs and the Art of Storytelling* (Syracuse University Press, 2014) and *The Blueness of the Evening: Selected Poems of Hassan Najmi* (University of Arkansas Press, March 2018). His poetry has appeared in *CELAAN* and *Poetry Ink Anthology*.

George Szirtes was born in Hungary in 1948 and came to Britain as a child refugee in 1956. His first collection, *The Slant Door*, was joint-winner of the Faber Prize in 1979. He has published many more since then, of which *Reel* won the T.S. Eliot Prize in 2004 for which he has been twice shortlisted since. His most recent collection is *Mapping the Delta* (Bloodaxe). He has been awarded various international prizes for his own poetry as well as for his translations of Hungarian poetry and fiction, including the Man Booker International translator's prize for his translations of László Krasznahorkai. He has written three books for children, most recently *How to be a Tiger* (2017). His memoir of his mother, *The Photographer at Sixteen* (2019), is published by MacLehose Press.

Jan Wagner was born 1971 in Hamburg and has lived in Berlin since 1995. Poet, essayist, translator (Charles Simic, Simon Armitage, Matthew Sweeney, Robin Robertson and others), he has published six poetry collections of poetry. A selection in English, *Self-Portrait with a Swarm of Bees*, translated by Iain Galbraith, was published in 2015 by Arc. He has received various awards, among others the Leipzig Bookfair Prize (2015) and the Georg Büchner Prize (2017).

Stefan Weidner was born in 1967. A German writer, translator and literary critic, he studied Arabic and Islamic Studies at the universities of Göttingen, Damascus, Berkeley (CA) and Bonn. He has published several volumes of fiction, travel writing and essays. Among the Arab authors he has translated are Adonis, Mahmoud Darwish and Ibn al-Arabi. From 2001 until 2016 he was editor-in-chief of *Art&Thought – Fikrun wa Fann*, a cultural magazine published in English, Arabic and Farsi (www.goethe.de/fikrun). His most recent book is *Jenseits des Westens. Für einen neuen Kosmopolitismus* (Beyond the Conceptions of the West. For a New Kind of Cosmopolitanism). His awards include the 2006 Clemens-Brentano Prize, the 2007 Johann-Heinrich-Voss Prize and the 2014 Paul-Scheerbart Preis. He is a member of the German Academy of Language and Poetry and a founding member of the Academy of the Arts of the World in Cologne.

Sibylle Wentker was born in Bonn in 1967 and studied Arabic, History and Turkology at the University of Vienna, Austria, receiving a PhD in Arabic Studies in 2002 with a dissertation on the Arabic *Physiologus* text. From 2005 she worked as librarian and researcher at the Institute of Iranian Studies, Austrian Academy of Sciences, and from 2014 she was additionally head of the Library, Archives and Collection of the Austrian Academy of Sciences. In August 2018 she was appointed Director of International Relations, Fellowships and Awards, and Research Funding at the Austrian Academy of Sciences. Her main research interests include the German translation of the *Tarikh-e Wassaf* by Joseph von Hammer-Purgstall, the intellectual history of European historiography concerning the 'Orient' (specifically Persia), Mamluk-Ilkhanid historiography and the history of Austrian-Iranian relations in the nineteenth century.

Shaun Whiteside was born in Co. Tyrone, Northern Ireland, in 1959. He has translated numerous books from German, French, Italian and Dutch, most recently the novels *To Die in Spring* by Ralf Rothmann, *Black Water Lilies* by Michel Bussi and *Malacqua* by Nicola Pugliesi, as well as works of non-fiction including *Swansong 1945* by Walter Kempowski, *Blitzed* by Norman Ohler and *Football* by Jean-Philippe Toussaint. He has taken translation workshops at the British Centre for Literary Translation, Birkbeck University and City University, and within the Emerging Translators programme organised by *New Books in German*, and has reviewed for journals including the *Guardian*, the *Observer* and the *Times Literary Supplement*. He lives in London with his family.

Frank Wynne was born in Sligo, Ireland, in 1962. He has been a literary translator for twenty years. The authors he has translated include Michel Houellebecq, Virginie Despentes, Tomás González and Javier Cercas. His work has earned him the IMPAC Prize (2002), the Independent Foreign Fiction Prize (2005), and he has twice been awarded both the Scott Moncrieff Prize and the Premio Valle Inclán. He has been translator in residence at Lancaster University, City University and the Villa Gillet, Lyon.

INDEX OF POETS AND ESSAYISTS

INDEX OF POEMS